American
Economic
Policy and
National Security

American
Economic
Policy and
National Security

Theodore H. Moran

COUNCIL ON FOREIGN RELATIONS PRESS

NEW YORK

COUNCIL ON FOREIGN RELATIONS

The Council on Foreign Relations, Inc., is a nonprofit and nonpartisan organization devoted to promoting improved understanding of international affairs through the free exchange of ideas. The Council does not take any position on questions of foreign policy and has no affiliation with, and receives no funding from, the United States government.

All statements of fact and expressions of opinion contained in Council books are the sole responsibility of the author.

If you would like more information about Council publications, please write the Council on Foreign Relations, 58 East 68th Street, New York, NY 10021, or call the Publications Office at (212) 734-0400.

Library of Congress Cataloging-in-Publication Data

Moran, Theodore H., 1943–
  American economic policy and national security / Theodore H. Moran.
     p. cm.
  Includes bibliographical references.
  ISBN 0-87609-137-0 : $10.95
  1. United States—National security—Economic aspects.
  2. United States—Economic policy—1981–   I. Title.
HC110.D4M66 1992
338.973—dc20   92–38843
                                                  CIP

93 94 95 96 97 98 99 EB 10 9 8 7 6 5 4 3 2 1

Cover design: Patrick Vittaco

CONTENTS

Foreword   vii

Acknowledgments   ix

Introduction   1

   I. The First Threat: Fundamental Economic
     Decline—*The Macroeconomic Dimension*   4

  II. The Second Threat: Loss of Crucial National
     Capabilities—*The Competitiveness Dimension* 13

 III. The Third Threat: Vulnerability to Delay,
     Denial, Manipulation, and Blackmail on
     the Part of External Suppliers—*The
     Dependence Dimension*   41

 IV. Conclusions: From Tactics, to Strategy,
     to Grand Strategy   70

Notes   82

About the Author   99

FOREWORD

The agenda for an American national security strategy has changed dramatically of late. Economics is coming to occupy a more prominent position in determining the capacity of the United States to lead others and influence events on the world stage. At the same time the mismanagement of economic policy carries threats and dangers to America's position in the international system.

In this study Theodore Moran examines three such threats: America's fundamental and cumulative decline in relation to the other major industrial states; a loss of crucial economic and technological capabilities within our own country; and the growing dependence on foreigners for goods, services, and technologies that are vital to our national well-being. In each area he explores the nature of the threat and analyzes the policy alternatives to meet it. In the end, however, Moran argues that the policy responses of greatest benefit to the United States cannot be selected according to economic criteria alone. Instead, American policymakers must construct what the author calls a "grand strategy" that derives from their vision of a structure for the international system that best serves American interests as well as their assessment of the ability of American political leaders to guide the public in ways that support this structure.

This essay is part of the Council's on-going effort to explore new dimensions of American national security in the aftermath of the Cold War. In this context *American Economic Policy and National Security* plays an especially useful role, connecting domestic concerns about economic issues with the broader question of American power and influence in the international arena. This study was funded by The Pew Charitable Trusts as part of the Project on America's Task in a Changed World administered by the Council on Foreign Relations.

Peter Tarnoff
President, Council on Foreign Relations

November, 1992

ACKNOWLEDGMENTS

I wish to acknowledge the support of the Council on Foreign Relations and the Pew Foundation in seeing this work through to completion. In addition, Business Executives for National Security, the global Security Project at Georgetown University, and the Center for Strategic and International Studies of Washington, D.C., have all supported research that has found its way into these chapters. My colleague Gary Hufbauer was one of many who provided insightful commentary and critique of these arguments. Finally, Myrna Young offered tireless assistance as I handed her draft after draft.

INTRODUCTION

How does the management of the domestic economy affect U.S. national security? What are the threats that mismanagement creates? Should the search for something entitled "economic security" be high on the agenda of American strategists as they confront an evolving world order?

There is a growing suspicion, not limited to Washington, that the great economic questions that affect America's position in the world, its ability to lead, its capacity to control its own destiny, are too important to be left to economists. These questions are:

- *Is the United States in decline as a great power?* Is the United States undergoing a process of cumulative economic deterioration vis-à-vis other industrial nations, or simply receding a bit from the exceptional position of supremacy it enjoyed in the first two decades after the devastation of Europe and Japan?

- *Will Americans end up "sweeping up" around Asian or European machinery?* Are the industrial successes of Japan or the European Community (EC-92) changing the structure of the American economy in ways that may come to haunt the United States in the future, or will the market provide outcomes that are satisfactory?

1

- *Computer chips, potato chips—what's the difference?* Does the globalization of the American industrial base carry genuine dangers of foreign dependency?

The discipline of economics arouses natural suspicion among those concerned with questions of national security. Its infatuation with consumer welfare, its indifference to the fate of producers, its agnosticism about the nationality of suppliers, its passion for international comparative advantage, and its scorn for relative rather than mutual gains do not appear to fit well with the goals of maximizing America's potency as a player among nations or of safeguarding the nation's standing against displacement by others.

Nonetheless, I shall argue that careful economic analysis can help us delineate the relationship between domestic economic policy and national security, specify the hazards of policy mismanagement, and provide guidelines for future behavior. Our first task is to identify the threats hidden in the changing shape of the international economy that American policy should be designed to counter or avoid.

This study focuses on three threats to America's ability to lead or influence others, in accord with its own values, and to behave autonomously: (1) fundamental and cumulative economic decline; (2) loss of specific economic and technological capabilities; and (3) dependence on external suppliers.[1] The three overlap but are conceptually distinct. Mixed among them are factors that are genuinely worrisome but can be corrected, factors that are mistakenly viewed with alarm and may be disregarded, and factors that are unavoidable but worthy of some insurance coverage.

Despite the economic basis of these threats, non-economic judgments must also guide policy. Some of the areas in which noneconomic judgments emerge are familiar: the choice, for example, between maximizing America's economic welfare and maximizing its political power (sacrificing mutual economic benefits to ensure an advantageous relative distribution of economic benefits, so as to enhance the nation's ability to influence others), or between maximizing economic welfare and minimizing the nation's vulnerability to being coerced by outsiders. Other areas in which noneconomic judgments come into play, however, will require some basic reconsideration of what constitutes national security in the new era. Besides the focus on national power, there are *systemic* considerations about the impact alternative domestic economic policies will have on the propensity for cooperation or antagonism among the major industrial nations themselves. The economic responses to the three threats cluster together in two alternative policy packages where the whole (in each case) is greater than the sum of its parts. The choice between them depends upon one's vision of the structure of the international system in the coming era and upon one's assessment of the ability of national leaders to guide their publics in ways that do not undermine that vision.

At the end of the day, therefore, a grand strategy that defines the kind of structure the United States would prefer for the international system, assesses the risks of moving toward one structure rather than another, and distributes the burden of payment between present and future generations must dominate the design of appropriate policies.

I

THE FIRST THREAT

Fundamental Economic Decline— The Macroeconomic Dimension

Is the United States undergoing a process of cumulative economic deterioration vis-à-vis other industrial nations, or simply receding a bit from the exceptional position of supremacy it enjoyed in the decades after the devastation of Europe and Japan? Colloquially, is the United States in decline as a great power?

The U.S. share of world output is declining, our productive lead is being eroded by faster-growing economies, the competitive position of our industries has weakened, our trade is in deficit, and our capital position has been transformed abruptly from net lender to net debtor—so writes Paul Kennedy in *The Rise and Fall of the Great Powers*. "It is instructive to note the uncanny similarities between the growing mood of anxiety among thoughtful circles in the United States today and that which pervaded all political parties in Edwardian Britain. . . . In terms of commercial expertise, levels of training and education, efficiency of production, standards of income and (among the less well-off) of living, health, and housing, the 'number one' power of 1900 seemed to be losing its position, with dire implications for the country's long-term *strategic* position." [2]

On the contrary, counters Joseph Nye, the extrapolation of decline from the most recent decades of American economic performance ignores the abnormal impact of World War II. Studies that allow for the recovery of Europe and Japan suggest that "the World War II effect lasted for about a quarter century and that most of the decline worked its way through the system by the mid-1970s and then stabilized." Much of the erosion of American preponderance since the 1950s is simply a "return to normal."[3]

This questioning of America's standing in the world system is not new. Samuel Huntington finds repeated phases of "declinism" in recent American history (five in the postwar era alone). Our preoccupations with decline, he concludes, may be "better indications of American psychology than of American power."[4]

Is the United States in decline or not? How can we know if America's position vis-à-vis its industrial rivals now rests in rough equilibrium, or is following a downward trajectory? Could the decline debate be simply another iteration of Huntington's phases, more a function of America's psyche than a reflection of the underlying reality?

A comprehensive assessment of America's place in the future world system could surely benefit from surveying centuries of comparative history (Kennedy), from including "soft power" resources of values and ideals (Nye), from psychoanalyzing America's view of itself (Huntington). In the end, a dynamic explanation of what propels a great power along one path or another might well depend on intuitive ponderings that would leave the national strategist with no concrete way to know until long after the fact, let alone measure from year to year or decade to decade, the answer to the question.

The Contribution of Macroeconomics
to the Decline Debate

The focal point for the economics discipline is just the opposite; it is simple, measurable, mundane in the extreme. To confront the challenge of analyzing whether the United States is undergoing a process of fundamental deterioration in its economic position relative to other nations, the natural starting place for economists is the relationship between consumption and savings in the United States in comparison to the corresponding ratio in its major industrial rivals. This approach does not pretend to account for all the facets of a great power in decline, but it does explain very clearly one key element, the direction of the trend in trade and capital flows (positive or negative), and predicts with some certainty how long an adverse trend will last. This, in turn, helps lay the basis for understanding the competitive position of American industries and the potential deterioration in the capabilities, economic and technological, to be found in the United States (Threat II), and, concomitantly, the growing susceptibility to foreign influence and foreign control (Threat III).

Drawing on the first lesson of Macroeconomics 101, this approach produces conclusions more dramatic than those of Paul Kennedy, more portentous than those of Joseph Nye, more concrete than those of Samuel Huntington, and different from all three. Its impact on policymakers, however, is usually not far different from the effect in the classroom—namely, a mix of confusion and sopor.

The most basic macroeconomic equations demonstrate that so long as the United States consumes more than it produces and does not save enough to finance new productive capacity to fill the consumption/production gap, there will be a trade deficit caused by the excess demand of U.S. consumers and capital inflows to make up for the deficiencies in savings. The trade deficit puts dollars into the hands of foreigners who treat them like IOUs, cashing them in over time to buy either products or assets (carrying the balance in the form of debt). Ultimately, the nation can pay off the amassed IOUs by expanding production in excess of domestic consumption or by selling off assets. The actual course of events, in which the United States evolves as a net seller of products or a net seller of assets, depends upon the consumption/savings ratio of others in comparison to ours. If we do not reduce our consumption and upgrade and enlarge the nation's production facilities with our own savings, foreigners will increasingly do it for us. But not in exact proportion: more likely is the troublesome combination of a weakly capitalized productive base, along with a steadily rising foreign accumulation of assets.[5]

Somber Implications

The implications of a high-consumption/low-savings ratio are profound: the deterioration in the trade and investment accounts will not stop until the ratio is altered. From the legacy of imbalance, moreover, national strategists face a future of fewer and fewer resources to meet national and international needs (as a rising proportion of domestic output must be dedicated to paying off accumulated debts), accompanied by a growing foreign presence in our midst.[6]

In this context, U.S. economic behavior has undergone in the last decade what in the glacial tectonics of macroeconomics constitutes a dramatic shift. According to the *Economic Report of the President*, from 1980 to 1990 consumption exceeded production by $1.2 trillion, creating trade deficits of approximately the same magnitude.[7] The trade deficits alone are not inherently "bad." If they had been accompanied by a high savings rate and if they had represented a vast inflow of capital equipment to renovate the economy, one could hope they would pay for themselves in new products and higher productivity. Instead, the trade deficit has been largely dedicated to satisfying consumer demand, mortgaging the country's future to finance current consumption. From 1980 through the early 1990s, gross national savings declined from 20 percent of GNP to 16 percent of GNP, reflecting a growth in the federal deficit (government dissaving), a decline in state and municipal surpluses, and a fall in private household and business savings.

Over the same period, the consumption and savings patterns of our major economic rivals, Germany and Japan, have been in many ways the mirror image, with production exceeding consumption by $954 billion, generating trade surpluses of the same magnitude. Their savings rates, meanwhile, have maintained an average of 23 percent and 32 percent of GNP, respectively. In the process, Europeans and Japanese have been compensating for some of the decline in American savings by doing it for us, reaching a high in the late 1980s of supplying approximately half of all our domestic investment.[8]

The meaning of this macroeconomic analysis for national strategy is somewhat counterintuitive to popular thinking: the fiercest Japan-bashing or EC-92–bashing in trade negotiations and the toughest "strengthening" of investment regulation via legislation like the Exon-Florio Amendment will not right the imbalances in trade and investment unless the underlying savings/consumption ratio in the United States is transformed. This arcane truth, accepted as gospel by the economics community, has been largely lost in the public policy debates. Macroeconomists convey an unpopular (and sometimes unwelcome) message when they declare that trade liberalization and foreign investment restrictions are not remedies in themselves: efforts on the part of a deficit country to achieve more openness from others and tighter closedness for itself can alter the composition of the nation's international imbalances but, in the absence of changes in the consumption/savings ratio, cannot change their magnitude. In a fundamental sense, our trade and investment deficits are indeed "Made in America."[9]

Furthermore, trade liberalization by other nations in response to U.S. demands may simply make them even more competitive in comparison to us as they incorporate productivity-enhancing products, including U.S. products—from microprocessors, to telecommunications switching gear, to cheap wheat and rice—into their economies.

Will Demographics Save Us?

Some will argue that an apocalyptic response to the deterioration of America's economic position over the past decade or so is unwarranted, given the shifting demographics of the Japanese and European populations in comparison to our own. Over time, the greater proportion of the elderly (who perforce consume more and save less than younger workers) in the Japanese and European societies might reestablish a balance in our trade and capital accounts.

But the aging population in Japan will not reach its crest until after 2020, in Europe only slightly earlier. Over the intervening years, the accumulation of dollar surpluses abroad will, by any historical measure, rise to massive proportions. The pressure of international market forces to spur exports—and force reductions in domestic consumption via almost certain devaluations of the dollar—will mean a steady decline in the American standard of living, and a declining capability to influence events on the world stage. The buildup of the foreign presence in U.S. economy that will occur along the way is difficult to estimate with anything resembling exactitude, but its dimensions (perhaps 30–40 percent of the capital stock)[10] could have much greater strategic implications for the United States than we can even imagine today (when foreigners own 10 percent of U.S. capital stock). Complacency about relying on demographic trends abroad to right macroeconomic disparities at home, therefore, leaves open a window of vulnerability for at least three decades.

Window of Vulnerability, Window of Opportunity

Broadly speaking, then, the contribution of macroeconomics to the decline debate comes out rather solidly on the affirmative side: the United States is set on a downward trajectory and, in the absence of fundamental behavioral changes, it will continue along this course. This conclusion differs, however, from Paul Kennedy's point of view and is in some ways even more gloomy. Kennedy blames the military expenditures that accompany "imperial overstretch" for the weakening of American economic performance. One might suppose, therefore, that the cutback in military spending engendered by the end of the cold war will help restore our economic health. But as the preceding macroeconomic analysis reveals, even if the United States cut back its political commitments and slashed its defense outlays (America could withdraw from East of Suez!), the cumulative decline of the United States will continue unabated if the resulting revenues go to consumption rather than investment. Much of Kennedy's analysis of the role of imperial overreach in the rise and fall of nations can be reduced, in fact, to a special case of the need to pursue macroeconomic stability, with military commitments being "excessive" (or not) only in relation to other kinds of consumption.[11]

Over the next quarter of a century or so, we may take some solace, as Joseph Nye does, in the fact that America's power and influence in the world system has a "soft," noneconomic, component, drawing on the appeal of our values and ideals. Even so, our ability to call on these unless they happen to fit with the national interests of others, or to persuade others by example, will surely grow more tenuous as the "hard" assets of economic resources (and the respect engendered by our ability to create them) diminish, especially if the track is steadily downward and the national will to reverse course is lacking.

Still, there is a bright side to this macroeconomic perspective. Although the analysis shows that, absent basic behavioral changes, the imbalances in trade and investment will persist, it also demonstrates that our economic fate is, to a considerable degree, in our own hands.

The coming decades therefore offer a window of opportunity to halt the process of cumulative decline or a window of vulnerability to witness the deterioration of American capabilities.

II

THE SECOND THREAT

Loss of Crucial National Capabilities—
The Competitiveness Dimension

Are the industrial successes of Japan and EC-92 changing the structure of the American economy in ways that may come to haunt the United States in the future, or will the market provide outcomes free from peril? More popularly, what steps are necessary to ensure Americans do not end up sweeping up around Asian or European machinery?

In the previous section I argued that fundamental decline (Threat I) cannot be avoided unless the United States makes the adjustments in the consumption/savings/investment ratio needed to restore the country to a rough equilibrium in its external accounts. But even if this threat were removed, and the U.S. economy returned to equilibrium, we might find rival states engaged in more productive, skill-intensive, technology-based activities. In stylized terms, the contrast will be between a high-productivity, high-value-added, high-wage, high-innovation equilibrium and a lower-productivity, lower-skill, lower-wage, less innovative, and less technology-intensive equilibrium.

Threat II emerges from this second kind of equilibrium, from a suboptimal or inferior set of activities in the worker-and-firm economic base that reduces a nation's capabilities in comparison to other states. The state with the inferior capabilities will have a lower standard of living than others; it will suffer adverse terms of trade (it will have to

13

exchange more of its own products for the ones it gets in return); and it will have fewer resources to deploy to meet external challenges, influence other states, or participate in common efforts in the international arena.

Even more worrisome, there could be extensive negative political externalities as countries looked elsewhere to deepen political relationships with those nations who were increasingly the providers of advanced products, the source of cutting-edge innovations, the locale of scientific breakthroughs. Finally, as the analysis of this issue reveals (below), the so-called equilibrium could itself be illusory, as dynamic effects from learning-by-doing and first-mover advantages were lost. Other nations could forge ahead in the most advanced high-tech sectors, with American firms struggling at a disadvantage to catch up. In this context, the United States would be increasingly vulnerable to being manipulated or denied access to the most advanced goods, services, and technologies (see the discussion of Threat III below), because of fewer offsetting dependencies on their part.

Consequently, an agenda for economic security must include the design of policies to influence what kinds of economic activities and productive capabilities are located within the country.

Strengthening U.S. Competitiveness

There are few more controversial issues than the question of shaping the composition of economic activity in the United States. Even use of the word "composition" invites trouble, threatening to plunge discussion toward doctrinal disputes about industrial policy.

What is remarkable is how much national strategists will be able to accomplish in addressing Threat II—in a way that satisfies economists' aversion to targeting and industrial policy advocates' special concern for the American industrial base—before having to confront the thorny questions of selective intervention or trade protection. Offering great comfort to the national strategist is the fact that, in contrast to the rather dismal contemporary context for addressing Threat I, the past decades have provided a powerful legacy of high-value-added, high-skill, high-innovation activities to build on in the present day. Although the United States (like Europe and Japan) is becoming more of a service economy, decreasing the *relative size* of the manufacturing sector ("the industrial base"), the *absolute size* of the manufacturing sector has been growing steadily larger and more technology-intensive. (Only the absolute size of the manufacturing labor force has shrunk slightly, consistent with increased automation.) At the same time, productivity in the U.S. manufacturing sector has risen noticeably, from an average gain of 2.6 percent per year in the 1960s through 2.3 percent in the 1970s, to 3.7 percent per year in the 1980s, giving American plants and workers the greatest output per unit of input in the world. Contrary to popular views, U.S. industrial workers are still the most productive in the world. The corresponding output of the Japanese worker in manufacturing is 83 percent of that of the U.S. worker, of the German worker 78 percent, and of the British worker 45 percent.[12] The American in-

TABLE 1.   U.S. MANUFACTURING OUTPUT
AS A PERCENTAGE OF GDP

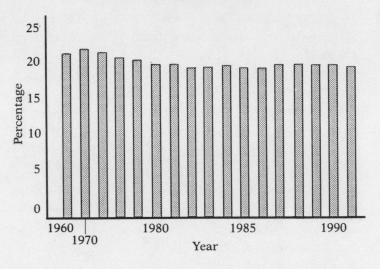

Source: Bureau of Labor Statistics (revised April 1992). Prior to 1977,
percentage of GNP is used. GNP measures output of a country's
firms wherever they are located; GDP measures the output of
firms within a country's borders.

dustrial base has grown both bigger and leaner in
the past three decades.

But has it grown meaner? To answer this question requires examining the competitiveness (comparative performance) of American firms and
workers with rivals elsewhere. Here the trends are
not favorable. Productivity growth in manufacturing in other nations has been rising even faster than
ours (although the foreign rate of growth is slowing).
Thus, compared to our competitors in Europe and
Asia, we have good reasons to be concerned.

What steps can the United States take to bolster
the productivity, dynamism, and innovativeness of

TABLE 2.   PRODUCTIVITY GROWTH IN MANUFACTURING

	United States	Japan	Germany
1960–70	2.6	10.3	5.7
1970–80	2.3	6.1	4.2
1980–88	3.7	4.5	5.7

Source: Department of Labor, Handbook of Labor Statistics

its industrial base? At first glance, the challenge of improving American competitive performance is surprisingly difficult. The task of isolating the determinants of productivity has led even the most careful analysts to throw up their hands. To a large extent, however, this is because of our blurred comprehension of what is going on in the service sector. When one looks at industrial activities directly, the diagnosis is more straightforward and easier to relate to the previous problems of macroeconomic policy.

The key elements to improving U.S. industrial performance are strengthening domestic investment in plant and equipment, strengthening domestic investment in human capital (worker education and training), and strengthening domestic investment in new technology.[13] The cost of capital is central to all three. For reasons largely related to the macroeconomic considerations discussed in the previous section, American firms have been operating at a substantial competitive disadvantage. The low U.S. savings rate (plus some tax considerations, to be discussed below) has translated into a higher cost of capital in the United States, a penalty of four to seven percentage points when compared to Japan

TABLE 3.   ALTERNATE ESTIMATES OF THE COST OF CAPITAL

	United States	Japan
Hatsopoulos-Brooks	9.7	3.8
McCauley-Zimmer	11.2	7.2
Bernheim-Shoven	11.1	4.1

Source: J. Poterba, "Comparing the Cost of Capital in the United States and Japan: A Survey of Methods," Federal Reserve Bank of New York, *Quarterly Review*, Winter 1991.

(with about half of this when compared to Germany) over the past two decades.

As a consequence, when U.S. or Japanese firms have contemplated the construction of a new plant or research facility, the American companies were stuck with having to spend three to eight times as much as their Japanese rivals over the 30-year amortization life of a proposed investment. When U.S. and Japanese firms have contemplated the payback period for comparable projects, the American companies have had to get their money back in eight years, compared to eighteen years for the Japanese companies (at 9 percent versus 4 percent interest rates). To be sure, prudent corporations everywhere will have a portfolio of projects with differing payback periods (some quite short term, some quite long term). But the differential in the cost of capital has afforded the Japanese or German firms considerable leeway that American firms do not enjoy.

One way to put U.S. firms on a more equal footing with their rivals abroad would be to eliminate the idiosyncratic American practice of taxing returns from corporate earnings twice. This means that corporate dividends should be tax free either to the provider (the firm) or to the recipient (the stock-holder). It also implies that accumulated corporate earnings as embodied in share appreciation should be tax free. But a larger remedial impact lies in increasing the pool of capital in the United States by altering the balance between savings and consumption.

Over time one might expect that the liberalization of capital markets will equalize the cost of capital across borders. On the other hand, restrictions in product markets and in the ability to acquire corporations (including hostile acquisitions) may keep capital markets effectively segmented.[14]

In the meantime, the competitive performance of American firms cannot help being affected by relatively weaker investment rates. Over the past decade, both Germany and Japan have been dedicating a larger percentage of GNP to investment in plants and equipment than the United States, and since 1989 Japan has begun to invest more *in absolute amounts* as well (even though the Japanese economy is approximately half as large as the U.S. economy).

The high cost of capital, moreover, explains much about the infamous short time horizons of American companies and suggests that the comparatively myopic perspective of the latter will not change until there is progress on the macro-economic front.[15]

Turning from the competitiveness of American firms to the competitiveness of American workers, one should recall that U.S. worker performance is the highest in the world and, measured by family efforts, there is scant evidence of comparative laziness in the American workforce. Whereas the individual Japanese worker, for example, greatly surpasses his (gender deliberate) U.S. or European counterpart in hours on the job and paucity of vacation days (2,100 hours per year versus 1,800 for Americans and 1,600 for Germans; 8 vacation days per year versus 20 for Americans and 30 for Germans), the American family is by most measures among the hardest working in the world (with multiple family members employed).[16]

Does the expansion of investment in human capital therefore promise the same potential improvement in performance that the expansion in physical plant and equipment might? At first glance, the challenge of improving worker performance might appear much more difficult because of the immensity of the problems that afflict America's K-12 educational system, and because of the received wisdom from twenty years of American education literature that more money does not help. Recent research suggests, however, that for the purposes of national strategists, neither is an accurate characterization of the challenge.

With regard to the question of whether additional investment in human resources will produce results, the received wisdom has traditionally suffered from a variety of statistical weaknesses, in particular the nonrandomness of test-taking. Straightforward comparisons of test results where there are large expenditures per pupil (Connecticut) with other regions where there are much smaller expenditures per pupil (South Dakota) have led to the conclusion that greater educational inputs do not do much to improve educational output. But since the population of those who produce test scores is a distinctive group whose size varies dramatically across locales, one ends up comparing the results from the top 2 percent in one state (South Dakota) with the results of the top 69 percent in another (Connecticut), imparting a sharp downward bias to the impact of public expenditures. When careful statistical adjustments are made for varying participation rates (and for demographic differences and for variation in school quality within states), there is much stronger justification for concluding that incremental resources devoted to smaller class size, higher teacher salaries, better facilities, do produce commensurate improvement in results.[17]

With regard to the immensity of overhauling America's educational structure, the subcomponent of the task of most immediate concern to national strategists here has shown itself to be far more manageable than reforming the system as a whole. In searching for institutions where worker skills are being most effectively transmitted, the rapidly growing universe of vocational courses in community colleges and private institutes offers impressive possibilities for enhancing worker productivity.[18] To the extent these "skill clinics" operate under pressures of the market on both the supply and the demand sides, they must design and update their curricula scrupulously to meet the most pressing employer needs. They cater to self-selected populations who do not lack career motivation or classroom discipline. Thus, while national strategists will not want to ignore the long-term need to upgrade America's K-12 educational system, they can take some comfort in the fact that public resources added at the margin in vocational training (including the last two years of high school followed by two years of postsecondary training) can produce palpable results. More broadly, the prospects for further innovation via national certification in ascending tiers of skill training throughout life (portable skill portfolios) appear quite promising from a comparative perspective. German (and other European) apprenticeship and craft programs suggest large potential gains when adapted to an American environment.[19]

Investing in Workers Versus Investing in Machines

The most effective (and highly leveraged) policy tool to sponsor improvement in worker productivity would be a corporate tax credit for education and training expenditures (partial reimbursement). This would ensure business involvement in the planning, execution, and updating of the curriculum; it would also provide an important synergism with capital investment and with corporate research and development (R&D). If only the latter receive public support, firms may find it rational to design production processes around worker deficiencies ("dumbing down" technology as fast food restaurants do by creating cash registers with pictures in place of numbers on the keys) rather than designing production processes to incorporate more highly skilled workers. Unless there are simultaneous incentives for investment in physical, technological, and human capital, national strategists should be wary of advice simply to let markets work.[20] American interests will not be served by settling into a highly automated low-skill equilibrium.

Finally, we should not overlook the need for adjustment assistance for workers. Trade adjustment assistance has both an economic and a political rationale.[21] Economically, it represents society's interest in assuring that domestic resources are redeployed as smoothly and rapidly as possible (while it is also motivated by humanitarian concerns for those dislocated by trade). Politically, it bribes those hit by the burden of adjustment not to use their political clout to halt the adjustment process. This latter rationale is not unimportant: while the benefits of trade liberalization typically outweigh the costs two to three times over, the costs are concentrated while the benefits are dispersed, meaning that textile workers or farmers or glassmakers may well be able to mount successful campaigns to block negotiations whose outcome the rest of society will greatly benefit from but not spend individual time fighting for (the Uruguay Round, the North American Free Trade Agreement), a classic case of the free-rider problem.

The problem with American programs of trade adjustment assistance in the past is that they did not motivate adjustment; instead they substituted for welfare ("burial expenses" in AFL-CIO parlance) with debilitating and humiliating consequences. Proposals for reform should help make trade adjustment assistance more effective in motivating workers to actually change jobs and locales rather than following the traditional pattern of simply sitting and waiting futilely for the old jobs to come back (providing 50 percent of the difference between a worker's old and new salary for two years, for example, effective only upon acceptance of a new job).[22]

To move from an assessment of the competitive position of U.S. firms and workers in the past to projections for the future, the relatively strong performance of the national industrial base has to be evaluated in light of the fact that it has been operating under an internally imposed burden. There is no way to judge precisely how well the United States economy would perform in comparison to the economies of other countries, if the burden were lifted. One can draw some inferences about the composition of activities, however, from the fact that American companies, supplying global industrial markets from diverse national sources, have been maintaining their relative market shares surprisingly well over the past two decades.[23] Moreover, as they have done this, they have not been hollowing out and abandoning their home country manufacturing operations as they moved offshore (a charge that Paul Kennedy and others level against English firms in explaining the industrial decline of Edwardian Britain). Instead, they have been upgrading local activities as a complement to overseas production; assets per employee in manufacturing operations of U.S. parent corporations have remained approximately 20 percent higher than in developed country affiliates and almost 200 percent higher than in developing country affiliates.[24] In the course of this outward expansion by American manufacturing multinationals, the share of the manufacturing base devoted to capital goods has risen in the aggregate from 28 percent to 38 percent, almost half of which is exported (double the proportion of the late 1960s).[25]

To the extent the new national strategists are able, therefore, to improve the production climate in America, one would expect American firms to expand and strengthen their industrial facilities within the United States (rather than, for example, simply speeding a new international division of labor in which service and administrative activities were centered in the United States). At the same time, of course, the United States would become an even more appealing locale for foreign investors (for the issue of whether their operations differ significantly from the operations of comparable U.S. firms, see below). As for the charge that nobody wants to buy American products, the reality is that the United States was the world's second largest exporter in 1990 (11.6 percent of the global total), behind Germany (12.1 percent), but well ahead of Japan (8.5 percent); preliminary indications suggest that America became number one in 1991.[26]

There is a dark side to this relatively upbeat economic assessment, however. A nation that does not invest in itself will not have as broad or as robust capabilities as one that does. At best, it will settle into a suboptimal equilibrium in comparison to the composition of economic and technological activities toward which a more frugal behavior pattern would lead it. In this context, the credo of maximizing consumer welfare needs to be infused with an ethic that transcends the immediate: the welfare of future generations is dependent upon a certain measure of restraint and discipline on the part of the present generation.

But is even this appraisal not too hopeful? Will the broad counsel to "simply practice responsible macroeconomics, and the market will take care of the rest"[27] prevent other countries from systematically capturing larger and larger shares of the high-productivity, high-skill, high-value-added, high-wage, high-innovation, technology-intensive activities at our expense? Can a doctrine of merely letting markets work ensure adequately against the threat of other nations undermining "the exercise of American power," in the words of a study of high-tech industries by the Berkeley Roundtable, and consequently laying "the basis of a wholly new system that could markedly reduce U.S. influence"?[28]

To pursue these questions, we cannot avoid the dilemmas of industrial policy and trade protection. What should national strategists extract from this debate?

The Debate over Industrial Policy

The early industrial policy debate that emerged in the mid-1980s took place in a peculiar context (expansionary fiscal policy, restrictionary monetary policy, high interest rates, and an overvalued dollar) that limited its applicability for future national strategy. Economists who wanted to let markets work were susceptible to charges of benign neglect (or worse) as one sector after another was decimated across the United States. Industrial policy advocates who urged immediate public intervention before the traditional sources of American economic strength were totally destroyed were susceptible to charges of wanting to replace the market entirely.

Now, as before, the starting point for economic analysis is that national interests are *not* served by selective intervention because markets are more effective in picking winners and losers than public officials and because interventionist measures penalize the rest of the economy (subsidies are a direct tax and trade protection an indirect tax on other activities). Selective intervention results in a less

productive, less competitive, less innovative composition of economic activities.

In contrast, the starting point for industrial policy analysis (putting aside strategic trade ideas for a
moment) is that national interests *are* served by
selective intervention because some sectors produce
beneficial spillovers for the rest of the economy
greater than those realized by the actors themselves,
meaning that the market fails to supply optimal
levels of resources to those sectors on its own.

In this contrast of perspectives, the question of
market failure looms large. Unless barriers to the
proper functioning of markets can be demonstrated,
the most logical intuitive justifications for industrial policy that appeared initially self-evident do
not hold up well to careful scrutiny: if the United
States wants even more high-skilled, high-value-
added industries, for example, so the early industrial policy argument went, why not simply target
such industries directly for public support?

But an industrial policy of reallocating investment toward high-value-added activities where the
capital/labor ratio ranges from three to six times
greater than elsewhere, without expanding aggregate investment, would simply generate unemploy-
ment and actually retard economic growth: the
given amount of capital as distributed among the
government-induced composition of economic activities would employ fewer workers.[29] National
strategists would therefore want to eschew intervention unless they were certain that the market was
failing to provide inputs to the targeted activities. In
general, however, the crucial demonstration of market failure has not been forthcoming.

Are there exceptions? What should national policy be where markets do fail to supply optimal amounts of resources to particular activities?

The clearest cases of market failure to emerge from the industrial policy debate lie along the cutting edge of creating new technologies and (equally important) the rapid incorporation of new technologies into commercial applications. Here, the beneficial spillovers to the nation from R&D activities run two to four times as large as the private return appropriated by the firms that undertake the R&D.[30] This "appropriability gap" justifies a role for public intervention to allocate larger resource flows for research and development than the market alone provides.

A Civilian Equivalent to DARPA?

Do these findings vindicate an industrial policy approach for R&D?

Contrary to the position of those who urge the creation of a governmental technology-targeting agency (a civilian equivalent to DARPA, the Defense Advanced Research Projects Agency), there is a straightforward way to fill this appropriability gap without encountering the pitfalls of having government bureaucrats try to pick winners and losers better than the market, namely, enlarging the R&D tax credit and making it permanent.[31] The tax credit would put an added impetus behind the industries for whom the payoff for extra R&D at the margin is greatest (according to one estimate, 432 firms in roughly eleven industries account for 80 percent of all privately funded R&D in the United States)[32] and speed the commercialization of the basic discoveries and innovations in which the U.S. scientific community excels. Moreover, putting incremental resources in the hands of the companies directly would help fund those externalities that come from investing in local communities, local infrastructure, local educational facilities, without having the play of politics dictating whether Palo Alto, Route 128, the Research Triangle, Rochester, or Chippewa Falls was the more deserving.

In the absence of a demonstration that public authorities (backed by scientific expertise) could focus and manage the selection process better than the companies who could benefit from the outcome, it is safe to say that, dollar for dollar, the R&D tax credit would produce superior results. Two separate studies have shown that federally funded research undertaken by U.S. firms has been demonstrably less productive than projects funded by the companies themselves.[33] As a consequence, even in the case of cutting-edge R&D, it is difficult to see how national strategists could emerge from looking at the evidence convinced of a need for broad programs of public micro-intervention in the U.S. economy. (As we shall see later, however, there may be a grander rationale for creating a civilian targeting agency for new technology, albeit a much more counterintuitive and controversial one than is commonly offered.)

But national strategists cannot get away from the industrial policy debate so easily. First they must confront some genuinely difficult arguments about strategic trade theory.

Strategic Trade Theory

Strategic trade theory, which focuses not simply on the industrial base in general ("manufacturing matters") but on specific types of industries where there are large economies of scale and great advantages from learning-by-doing, breathed new life into the industrial policy debate.[34] Such industries, including aerospace, advanced materials, computers and supercomputers, semiconductors, and biochemicals, have grown up around the world through a combination of historical circumstance, public support, and local investment in human and physical infrastructure in a manner only loosely related to inherent factor endowments in a region or country. By providing public support for such industries, the strategic trade literature argued, perhaps states could genuinely "create their own comparative advantage" in a way not envisioned in traditional trade models.[35]

Reinforcing the case for public sector intervention, from the perspective of national strategists, economies of scale mean that global markets will only sustain a given number of production sites, and the dynamic acquisition of skills in the course of production means that countries which miss one generation of products may have grave difficulties in fielding participants in the next generation. Under such conditions, it is not hard to make a convincing argument that national authorities will want to ensure the presence of national players in these key industries. Simply sitting by passively and allowing the market to work, in contrast, might be dangerous;

it could leave the nation too far behind to be able to catch up with more activist rivals abroad.

The objections to turning U.S. policy in the direction of strategic trade interventionism come, in the first instance, not from theoretical flaws in the justification but from practical considerations of implementation. (For the theoretical flaws themselves, including other nations' reactions, the prisoners' dilemma, and potential escalation, see below.)

The first practical difficulty springs from the fact that while there is an intuitive sense that such externalities are inherent in many advanced industries, there are no clear indicators of market failure (once again) for targeteers to use to guide public funding. Without clear indicators, how should government bureaucrats sort through potential candidates? Should industries with especially high profits get extra help from the government? Or industries with low profits? Industries with exceptionally well-paid workers? Or industries with low-paid workers? Confining the focus to high-tech sectors, why semiconductors but not opto-electronics? What about supercomputers, synthetic materials, or agrichemicals? And within sectors, how can government officials choose among technical alternatives?

Laying aside a historical record in which the ability of bureaucrats to pick winners and losers better than the market has never been very good, the two so-called test cases for strategic trade-type targeting, supercomputers and high definition television (HDTV), have tended to confirm that decentralized market-driven processes of economic selection are in fact superior to centralized designation (even when the much vaunted Japanese targeting apparatus provides the designation).[36] The very existence of such test cases, moreover, has been the exception rather than the rule in overcoming the political clout of already-established losers; in the battle for public resources, sunset has proved more popular than sunrise on the horizon of the industrial democracies.[37]

Reinforcing the pessimism on the practical level, the record of government intervention on behalf of favored industries has confirmed that the handiest tools of public support are likely to be the most counterproductive. Rather than the (relatively speaking) less distortionary use of on-budget subsidies, public authorities have consistently preferred off-budget solutions via trade protection. Moreover, the form of trade protection itself—quantitative restrictions rather than tariffs—has (while offering some financial support to targeted industries such as machine tools, semiconductors, and steel) generated much larger trade rents that flow to their rivals abroad, allowing the latter to upgrade and prepare a stronger assault for the next round of competition. Meanwhile, the domestic users of semiconductors and machine tools, such as U.S. supercomputer and aerospace companies, suffer from high input costs that leave them at a disadvantage as well in comparison to their foreign competitors.[38]

The 1986 Semiconductor Agreement has been a sobering experience. The United States ended up creating a global cartel, under the supervision of Japan's Ministry of International Trade and Industry (MITI), to keep the prices of semiconductors high for the benefit of producers but with a devastating impact on any user who did not have a captive source of supply (as most U.S. users, in contrast to the Japanese, did not). As David Mowery and Nathan Rosenberg conclude, if the results of the 1986 Semiconductor Agreement are considered a success, it is hard to imagine what would constitute a failure.[39]

Thus, after a decade of contention, the outcome of the industrial policy debate leaves national strategists in a quandary: they are faced with appealingly rigorous justification for activism in crucial industries, namely, high-tech industries with large economies of scale and dynamic learning-curve advantages; but the prospects of creating an effective national policy are poor.

Is there not some less ambitious interventionism possible to ensure that American firms in strategic trade-type industries have an adequate place in global markets? Should not the United States be hypersensitive, at the least, to the potentially preemptive and predatory actions of others?[40] Otherwise, America's rivals may capture a lopsided number of a given set of desirable jobs and industrial activities and use them as a springboard to gain greater and greater shares in the future.

"America's rivals," of course, tends to mean Japan. Between 1970 and 1987, Japan's share of global exports of science-based industries doubled, from 8 percent to 16 percent of the world total, while the U.S. share fell from 29 percent to 20 percent (and the EC share likewise declined from 45 percent to 38 percent).[41] But, whereas most countries exchanged access to each other's domestic high-tech markets in the process, Japan remained singularly self-contained. In contrast to both Germany and the United States, there was no discernible movement toward

TABLE 4.   DOMESTIC SHARE OF HOME MARKET
IN HIGH-TECH GOODS

	Germany	Japan	United States
1970	77	94	95
1980	59	93	89
1985	43	94	84

Source: National Science Board, Science and Engineering Indicators, 1989.

opening. Japan's own behavior justifies classifying it as an outlier. In practice, argue Robert Kuttner and Clyde Prestowitz, America's adherence to an ideology of nonintervention makes our economic fate the captive of other nations' industrial strategies.[42] The proper fallback position, according to this argument, is to fashion trade policy into a kind of substitute for industrial policy.

Trade Policy as Industrial Policy

The objectives of trade-policy-as-industrial-policy would be to ensure that American high-tech producers are not unfairly shut out of foreign markets and that foreign high-tech producers do not engage in unfair behavior that drives American companies out of the U.S. domestic market. In addition, to address the requirements of strategic trade-type industries (to be precise, industries in which economies of scale require markets larger than single countries and in which producers gain learning-curve advantages that enable them to leapfrog over each other from one generation of products to another—not merely whatever industry politicians or interest groups choose to label "strategic"), a third objective takes on crucial importance: to ensure that the United States gets rapid results, not merely long-term promises.

We might ask ourselves what is new about this approach, since the multilateral GATT negotiations already pursue the first two objectives. But the GATT outcomes are slow and uncertain. In high-tech industries, argues Laura D'Andrea Tyson, "slow resolution of trade policy disputes can be potentially disastrous to American firms or industries."[43] In strategic trade theory, the third objective, a results-oriented desire for speed and certainty comes to drive the entire trade-policy-as-industrial-policy approach.

To pursue the goal of ensuring American producers are not shut out of foreign markets, conventional trade negotiations attempt to establish rules requiring that price, quality, and technical performance be the only criteria for awarding contracts. Bound by such rules, national (and local) authorities would have to follow nationality-blind purchasing practices.[44]

In the results-oriented critique, the quest for a rules regime (however appealing to Anglo-Saxon ways of thought the latter may be) is far too idealistic to meet the needs of strategic trade-type industries. To ensure rapid results in trade that involves a relatively small number of large, sensitive transactions (e.g., aircraft, supercomputers, satellites, telecommunications equipment) in which government purchases or government-directed purchases constitute a large percentage of all sales,[45] the pursuit of nationality-blind procurement procedures pales in comparison to the dependability and dispatch of bilateral negotiations that set numerical targets, pledges, or quotas, sector by sector; in short, in comparison to the alternative of some kind of managed trade.

To guard against foreign producers engaging in predatory behavior that drives American companies out of their own domestic markets (or out of any other markets), conventional trade negotiations aim to establish a discipline that enables all parties to compete fairly, with no firm receiving unfair government subsidies or selling for prices that are unfairly low (dumping). On the issue of subsidies, a level playing field necessitates agreement on a common formula and common ceiling for assistance from defense budgets, and requires that regional, state, and municipal support be submitted to multilateral constraints.[46] With regard to dumping, any attempt to level the playing field for strategic trade-type industries must adjust to the forward-pricing practices that are inherent in industries in which costs drop sharply with the lengthening of production runs and the accumulation of learning-curve experience (a 20 percent to 40 percent cost reduction with each doubling of output in chemicals, semiconductors, and aircraft, for example), rendering inappropriate a rule forbidding sales below the average of previous per-unit costs.[47] A new, and more suitable, standard of fair pricing, in turn, would have to rest on much closer antitrust coordination and enforcement across borders, in which the structure of a given industry and the predatory intent of the pricer were given thorough scrutiny.

As the history of GATT negotiations has illustrated, progress in achieving more harmonized standards on subsidies and on dumping is not impossible. But what is certain, argue those who want to use trade-policy-as-industrial-policy, is that here again the process of achieving concrete results will be anything but swift.

Bilateral Arm-Twisting and Managed Trade

Thus, as national strategists attempt to assess the trade-policy-as-industrial-policy argument, the criticism of the pace of progress on the issues of greatest concern for strategic trade-type industries stands well founded. But specifying a preferable alternative that will serve the interests of American national strategists is more difficult. To ensure market penetration, the counterproductive outcome of the 1986 Semiconductor Agreement has spurred experiments with "voluntary" import expansion agreements (in a VIE agreement a minimum share of a given national market is allocated to foreigners) to take the place of restraints on exports.[48] But all such attempts to carve up national markets have important anticompetitive effects (VIEs, for example, require government cartelization to apportion the promised import quantities and are likely to rest on trade diversion in favor of the strong-arm country at the expense of all others). More worrisome, experimentation with carefully contrived versions of managed trade on strategic-industry grounds opens the door to cruder efforts to divide up markets. And, once the door is open, it will be hard to shut (politically or legally) against the pleas of other industries that lack the structural characteristics which might in theory justify such an exceptional approach (if microelectronics qualify, why not consumer electronics, auto parts, autos themselves, even agricultural products?). Finally, whether sophisticated or crude, attempts to manage trade fall back on bilateral arm-twisting rather than multilateral agreements founded upon mutual concessions, a practice that is bound to leave a legacy of resentment on the part of those whose arms are twisted and those whose trade is diverted when the twister is successful.

In the case of dumping, the results-oriented approach has led to a proliferation of arbitrary penalties, defensible neither in strategic-trade terms nor according to GATT rules. The method of procedure, in both European and American practice, has been to appoint oneself judge, jury, and executioner in specifying what constitutes unfair practices (including many not considered unfair by GATT), deciding the innocence or guilt of the other parties, and resorting to the threat or actual imposition of nationally determined punishment to force compliance with one's own verdict.[49]

Similarly, in the case of subsidies, attempts to define acceptable behavior in strategic trade-type industries has also grown more unilateral and capricious, a trend that the proliferation of public programs to promote civilian R&D will doubtless exacerbate. (The EC has already shown that it can be even more flagrant in playing the aggressive unilateral game on subsidies and dumping than we can.)[50]

Taken altogether, therefore, the extent to which a shift to a trade-policy-as-industrial-policy results-oriented approach will actually serve American economic interests, even the narrow subcategory of interests clustered around the special needs of American strategic trade-type industries, is problematic. Not at all problematic, however, is the likelihood that the results-oriented approach will generate political tension among the major players since "progress" is built on unilateral definitions of fairness, bilateral pressure, and threats of retaliation rather than on the tradition of mutual concessions and multilateral negotiations that has characterized trade policy since the end of World War II.

Reinforcing concern about political tensions, there is an escalatory impulse along this path that may prove hard to mute: the use of trade-policy-as-industrial-policy to ensure that other nations do not capture a lopsided share of the most vital industries and that one's own country is represented adequately carries an inherent beggar-thy-neighbor dynamic. Global economies of scale may mean that not every major country can field a viable player. In the course of determining which nations (or groups of nations) will have to do without, what are time-urgent pressures for some are time-urgent pressures for all. The logical response in a duel of strategic trade policies is to match or exceed the first actor's moves to guard against preemption. Under such (prisoners' dilemma) conditions, a stalemate and cease-fire in which all sides regrouped to search for common agreement on underlying rules might become greatly to be wished for. At this point, the actors might well ask why they did not press even more vigorously for a rules-oriented outcome *before* the outbreak of hostilities.

The task for American national strategists, therefore, is to weigh the risk of erosion of indigenous capabilities in strategic trade-type high-tech industries under our traditional rules-oriented multilateral approach toward trade negotiations (with renewed determination but admittedly slow-moving advances) against the risk of rising international antagonisms and quite possibly counterproductive economic results under a results-oriented approach.

III

THE THIRD THREAT

Vulnerability to Delay, Denial, Manipulation,
and Blackmail on the Part of External Suppliers—
The Dependence Dimension

*Does the globalization of the American industrial base carry genuine
dangers of foreign dependence? More popularly, computer chips,
potato chips—what's the difference?*

Viewed from the perspective of Threat II (the loss of
national capabilities), the choice between computer
chips and potato chips might be surprisingly close.
If one takes potato chips to be indicative of a robust
agribusiness industry (instead of merely a vacuous
product with no redeeming value), most national
strategists would consider themselves fortunate to
have strong domestic strengths there, as well as in
semiconductors.[51]

Viewed from the perspective of Threat III (dependence), however, the question becomes what to
do when a country does not have indigenous competitive capabilities in both. A Japanese national
strategist might well ask, "Electronic products, food
products—what's the difference?" and conclude (on
the basis of Japan's history) that any possibility of
being denied food products (or of being vulnerable
to blackmail via a threat of a cut-off of supply) would
pose the greater danger to the nation. The determination of which is the more serious threat, denial of
food products or denial of electronic products, is an

41

empirical question that rests on the credibility of facing a hypothetical cut-off, on the time and difficulty of developing alternatives, and on the potential for creating stockpiles. Such considerations are the starting place for dealing with the challenge of dependency.

No matter how successful American efforts are to address Threats I and II, the United States will become more dependent in the future. Even if macroeconomic policies were in long-term balance, and even if (backed by strong investment flows into plants, equipment, education and training) all American workers and firms were operating with maximum efficiency and high innovation, the globalization of the U.S. industrial base would continue. That is, we will continue to rely on foreign providers for a growing proportion of the goods, services, management, and technologies we use. The idea of the United States enjoying technological and productive predominance in every sector is more than a historical anomaly, it is a logical impossibility: no nation can have a comparative advantage in everything.

How far will the process of globalization go? There is no basis on which to predict where a natural stopping place might be as technological prowess spreads more evenly around the world. As a point of reference, we are likely to continue to head in the direction of, say, Germany, where more than 57 percent of all high-tech goods, for example, are produced by foreigners (as compared to 16 percent currently in the United States).

In conventional economic analysis, globalization does not represent a failure; it represents a success. To be sure, no nation has ever wanted to be at the mercy of outsiders for industries vital to national defense, and this has given rise to an agonizing dilemma between autarchy and efficiency. But, in the course of history, autarchy has been reserved for only the narrowest classes of finished weapons systems (ships, artillery) since the autarchic route is not only expensive but leads rapidly to economic and technological (and therefore political) inferiority.[52] Today, however, there is a much broader array of military, commercial, and dual-use goods, services, and technologies whose provision is spread internationally.

The Trade-Off between Efficiency and Autarchy

How can one identify where there is a genuine threat in this process and where there is not? National strategists cannot avoid wrestling anew with the ancient problem of dependence on foreigners and working through, once again, the trade-offs between autarchy and efficiency.

For the United States, a rich resource base, strong indigenous scientific prowess, and exposed sea lanes of communication have combined to keep the idea of self-sufficiency alive as a touchstone of national policy. Even in today's critical-technology proposals, there is a certain wistfulness for Fortress America, where the United States avoids dependence on outsiders by being self-reliant for every cutting-edge product and process. But high-tech autarchy, like other kinds of autarchy, is increasingly costly, inefficient, and ultimately infeasible as technological prowess spreads around the world.

Providing some comfort in these circumstances, in an era in which there is a vanishing probability of protracted wartime disruption of supply lanes, national strategists are freed to direct their attention to that narrow subcategory of dependence where deliberate denial on the part of the supplier (or the supplier's home government) is a credible possibility.

Here there is an analytic tool that vastly simplifies the task for national strategists: the necessary condition for deliberate denial to be credible is the concentration of global markets. The threat hidden in the globalization of the industrial base springs today not from the *extent* of dependence on outsiders, therefore, but from the *concentration* of dependence on a few foreign suppliers where substitutes are few, the lead time to develop alternatives is long, and stockpiling is not feasible. Only within this much diminished set of circumstances can the commercial suppliers themselves threaten to manipulate the flow of goods, services, or technology to users in the United States, or in the extreme, become channels for blackmail, denial, or other forms of extraterritorial diktat on the part of foreign powers.

This perspective is, in general, greatly liberalizing, as national strategists look to the future. Most dependence on foreign suppliers does not matter and can safely be ignored. But where foreign suppliers are concentrated, it cannot.

The apprehensions caused by the concentration of foreign suppliers is not merely hypothetical. History is full of attempts by governments to influence the sovereign activities of other nations by withholding supplies or issuing extraterritorial directives to the overseas affiliates of domestic firms.[53] The United States itself has attempted to exercise such coercive power—witness the instructions from American authorities to IBM to have its French subsidiary withhold computer technology from France in the 1960s in order to inhibit de Gaulle's development of an independent nuclear deterrent; or, more recently, the Reagan administration's unilateral and retroactive order to the European subsidiaries of Dresser Industries and General Electric to cancel their contracts to supply technology for the Soviet gas pipeline. Other countries have shown a similar propensity to use their international companies as vehicles for external diktat. It is worrisome to contemplate that our country may increasingly be on the receiving end of such extraterritorial mandates.

In the economic sphere, 42 percent of a sample of U.S. firms interviewed by the General Accounting Office in 1991 reported, for example, that Japanese suppliers had rejected their requests to purchase advanced goods, parts, or technologies or had delayed their delivery by more than six months.[54] Nor is the political dimension of denial absent in the American encounter with industrial globalization. In the future, we may face more experiences like the Kyocera case, in which MITI (under antinuclear pressure from Socialist members of the Japanese Diet) forced Dexcel, the American subsidiary of Kyocera, to withhold its advanced ceramic technology from the U.S. Tomahawk missile program. Ironically, with the decline of cold war solidarity, an expanding number of political groups in the legislatures of our allies may enjoy increasing leeway to deny us access to technology or to set conditions for its use in the decades to come.

The threat of (credible) denial or manipulation leads to legitimate national security exceptions to

liberal doctrines of free flows of trade and investment. To specify where the exceptions occur, there is
a useful empirical finding from antitrust studies
that can provide a guideline for policy: if the largest
four firms (or four countries) control less than 50
percent of the market, they lack the ability to collude
effectively even if they wish to exploit or manipulate
recipients. If they control more than 50 percent of
the market, they do hold the potential to coordinate
denial, delay, blackmail, or manipulation. This
"four-four-fifty rule" provides an objective test of
whether a genuine threat to national security exists.[55]

National Security Exceptions
to Free Trade

In the trade arena, the concentration test would
apply equally to all the products of struggling industries that appeal for blanket trade protection on
national security grounds[56]—to footwear (since sol-
diers do require boots to march), as well as to machine tools, ball bearings, and steel.

To illustrate the difference between dependence that is genuinely worrisome and dependence
that is not, one might consider a political advertisement sponsored by the Fiber, Fabric, and Apparel Coalition.

The coalition was trying to gain trade protection for domestic makers of boots, uniforms, and
helmets to avoid U.S. dependence on outsiders for
these crucial items. What is analytically askew is
not that boots, uniforms, and helmets are unimportant, but rather that their provision is so dispersed
that sustained, deliberate denial on the part of the

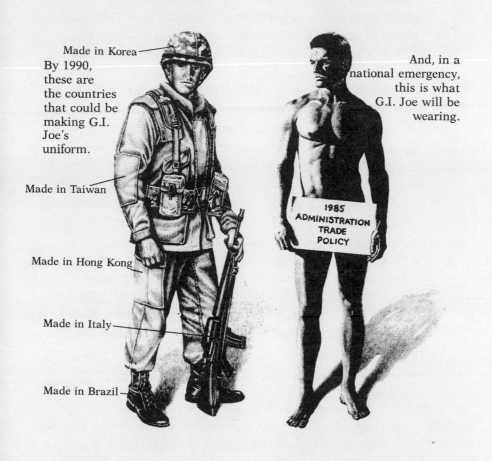

Made in Korea

By 1990, these are the countries that could be making G.I. Joe's uniform.

Made in Taiwan

Made in Hong Kong

Made in Italy

Made in Brazil

And, in a national emergency, this is what G.I. Joe will be wearing.

1985 ADMINISTRATION TRADE POLICY

Source: Washington Post, November 21, 1985, page A23.

FIGURE 1   ADVERTISEMENT FROM THE FIBER, FABRIC, AND APPAREL COALITION FOR TRADE

suppliers is not credible (the purchaser would simply shift orders to alternative sources). To be fair, the advertisement was first inaugurated in the mid-1980s when submarine attacks on convoys carrying boots from Brazil might have been conceivable, but even then stockpiling, rather than trade protection, would have been the more efficient remedy.

Following the logic of concentration being the necessary condition for denial, no longer would it make sense to protect domestic producers of items whose suppliers are widely dispersed internationally, no matter how critical the provision of supplies was claimed to be, even if the last domestic producer were threatened with extinction. Conversely, there would be a legitimate case to grant a national security tariff (or a subsidy, which is more efficient, if the fiscal and political system would support it) to domestic producers of crucial products whose provision from abroad is in the hands of a few suppliers.[57]

Turning to other examples of sectors that have frequently appealed for trade protection with an explicit or implied national security rationale, the machine-tool, ball-bearing, and steel industries are not sufficiently concentrated that denial on the part of external suppliers is a credible worry. Trade protection for any one of these entire industries, therefore, is unwarranted on national security grounds. At the same time, however, some narrow segments of the machine-tool industry might qualify—multi-axis cutters and grinders, and non-metallic shapers, for example, appear to be particularly concentrated; so too might portions of the ball-bearing industry, or some specialty steels. As in all trade cases, how much of a given industry might have to be covered for the target subsectors to remain viable is an empirical question: some concentrated subsectors might not be able to survive with mere niche production, in which case extensive protection would be appropriate.[58] In general, however, the presence of large flows of intra-industry trade demonstrates that a nation seldom has to host an entire industry for many segments to enjoy the economies of scale needed to compete in international markets.[59]

Overall, this approach to trade policy would place strict limitations on future appeals for trade protection. The formula is: no global concentration, no possibility of foreign "control," no threat to American national interests.

Gone would be comprehensive protection of entire industries, which saddles all users with higher input costs. Gone would be grossly distortionary protectionist measures (quantitative restrictions). Gone, too, would be efforts to prop up domestic producers in ways that reward foreign producers with trade rents (VRAs and VERs). Most important, if adopted as the standard around the globe, this approach would subject trade actions taken in the name of national defense to the discipline of an objective test, instead of to the intuitive sentiment of the would-be protector as prevails today.

Finally, this carefully targeted tariff protection (or subsidy) would not only promise enhanced viability to the current owners of the crucial concentrated facilities but also stimulate the interest of potentially superior domestic acquisitors. It would simultaneously attract foreign companies to set up local operations. These are features of considerable importance as one turns to the consideration of foreign investment.

National Security Treatment of Foreign
Acquisitions: Who-Is-Us? Revised

The optic of global concentration helps the national strategist sort through the issue of what the Defense Science Board has labeled the "penetration" of the domestic industrial base via foreign direct investment, including through the acquisition (friendly or hostile) of American firms. Today the oversight procedures of the U.S. government are opaque and confused: it is often more difficult for an overseas company to buy an American product containing sensitive technology than it is to purchase the entire company that makes the product.

As a general proposition, of course, foreign direct investment provides inputs of technology, management, and capital to the U.S. economy that help it become more productive. National strategists will want to support inward investment by foreigners for the same reasons that we encourage Europeans, or Canadians, or Mexicans, or Japanese to do the same. To be sure, American strategists will want to know whether direct investment by foreigners behaves significantly different from domestic firms with regard to skill-intensity of the jobs, amount of R&D, procurement practices, labor relations, and the like. One would want to be satisfied (for reasons associated with Threat II) that foreign investors did not keep the best jobs and research activities solely for home-country operations or, worse, take over indigenous companies and restructure operations so as to siphon off the most prized functions for headquarters. The initial indications are that this does not occur, that there are no major, systematic differences in behavior between local firms and affiliates of foreign companies when type of industry is held constant.[60] But is this type of surveillance enough?

To the extent that foreign investors conduct their operations like domestic companies but generate superior performance, observers such as Robert Reich question the importance of firm nationality, as measured by ownership of the stock or the citizenship of the board of directors or location of parent headquarters. All that need concern national strategists, according to this line of analysis, is whether any given corporation can improve the effectiveness of the workforce and strengthen the competitiveness of the local economy. "So who is us?" asks Reich. "The answer is, the American work force, the American people, but not particularly the American corporation."[61] Within the horizon of concerns of Threat II (ensuring domestic capabilities), this stance would lead to unreserved welcome for any and all foreign contestants in the domestic market.

But, again, the issue of concentration arises: without examining with some care the instances in which there are a shrinking number of suppliers, such a stance might be too nonchalant. Here we could find ourselves so dependent on goods, services, and technologies controlled by foreign-owned companies in the United States that our country would have to follow conditions laid down by outsiders to use their inputs or, in the extreme, to ask permission to pursue policies needed to advance our own national interests around the world.

The area of most concern is foreign investment via acquisition (46 percent of the cases and 79 percent of the value, according to the most recently available data), where, in the late 1980s, there were more than 400 takeovers in the microelectronics, aerospace, telecommunications, and advanced materials sectors alone.[62] A case in point involved the proposed takeover of a maker of advanced lithography equipment to imprint circuit patterns on silicon wafers in the semiconductor industry. The producers of this equipment ("steppers") are so few in number that they possess quasi-monopoly power. The acquisition of an American stepper manufacturer by a foreign company (as Nikon proposed with Perkin Elmer) would open the door to a kind of dependence for the United States that could be preyed upon by the parent corporation or the parent corporation's government.[63]

For the array of civilian and defense-related technologies in which suppliers might be similarly concentrated, the conditions imposed by outsiders could range from discrimination by use (no nuclear applications), to discrimination by destination (no sales to Israel), to discrimination with regard to commercial activity (permission required to re-export), to discrimination with regard to discrimination (no denial of sales to Iran)—all potentially subject to unilateral retroactive determination (requiring the United States to face what the Europeans experienced with the Soviet gas pipeline case in reverse).

As in the case of trade, the challenge is to devise a workable policy toward acquisitions of U.S. firms by outsiders when global markets are dominated by tight foreign monopolies or oligopolies. Once again, the use of a concentration measure offers a simple and effective method to strengthen CFIUS (Committee on Foreign Investment in the United States) procedures through which the U.S. government monitors foreign takeovers: if a foreign acquisition is proposed in an industry where concentration is higher than four companies or four countries supplying 50 percent of the global market, the U.S. government should impose performance requirements on the acquiring firm to ensure the retention of operations in the United States; if a foreign acquisition is proposed in an industry where concentration is lower than four companies or four countries supplying 50 percent of the global market, the U.S. government should approve the acquisition without conditions.

Strengthening the CFIUS screening mechanism with a concentration test has the advantage of avoiding the need to reopen the debate over industrial policy. The approach outlined here does not depend upon the dubious ability of government bureaucrats to pick winners and losers better than the market. Instead, it is based on established principles of aversion to monopolistic or oligopolistic power that have always guided the American preference for free markets.

Why not follow the Fortress America impulse, and simply block foreign acquisitions in globally concentrated industries altogether?

All else being equal, if there is a "national solution" available to sustain the target firm as a world-class competitor, either by channeling additional resources to the company (via a tariff or a subsidy) or by having other domestic corporations acquire the firm, the threat of external manipulation may be obviated by blocking the foreign purchase. If the foreign acquisitor possesses superior technology or product expertise, however, the pursuit of a national solution via tariff, subsidy, and/or domestic buy-out may simply prop up a second-rate local producer while leaving the potentially superior foreign supplier in the globally concentrated industry offshore. The performance requirement route, in contrast, actively induces foreign firms in sensitive concentrated industries to carry out research and production within American jurisdiction to mitigate the threat of delay, denial, or manipulation from offshore.[64]

As technological capabilities spread more widely around the globe, the number of cases in which a competitive national solution can be found will inevitably shrink. On balance, for concentrated civilian and dual-use products and technologies, perhaps the benefit of the doubt should be given to allowing the acquisition to proceed with the performance requirements in place, and the burden of proof that a "national solution" would be superior should be laid on those who would oppose the acquisition.

The Most Difficult Case: Acquisition of Defense Companies by Foreign Allies

The proposed acquisition of a domestic defense company by a foreign corporation adds another dimension to the dilemmas noted above. The acquisition of a defense company is different from the acquisition of a critical civilian or dual-use supplier in that it requires some special precautions to protect against disclosure of classified information. These special precautions include voting trusts, proxy arrangements, and special security agreements whose objective is to isolate the foreign owners from the operations of the U.S. affiliate sufficient to ensure against unauthorized access to sensitive, compartmented, or top secret information and technologies. Under such arrangements, the foreign owner distances itself from direct contact with information that must be handled by cleared U.S. citizens.

As we can see from the preceding analysis, however, a preoccupation with protection against disclosure of classified information is too narrow. It leaves open the question of maintaining control over the disposition of the subsidiary's output if there is a conflict of national directives from home and host governments.

What is needed is a broader methodology for CFIUS review procedures that will apply equally to the proposed acquisition of defense contractors, as well as to the proposed acquisition of civilian firms with critical technologies. The following decision chain sketches out a single sequence to apply to both:

First, once again, strategists must consider the issue of concentration, or how wide a range of comparable products or technological substitutes exist. Here, one can imagine instances where there are many defense suppliers of equipment, electronics, (even) weapons, or contrary instances where there are few equivalent goods or services.

Second, in cases where the range of substitutes is narrow, national strategists must appraise the likelihood that the home government of the prospective parent corporation might impose directives on the company which conflict with the interests of the American host (in the extreme, becoming antagonistic or hostile to the United States).

Third, as the decision chain in Figure 2 illustrates, in cases where the range of substitutes is narrow and the likelihood of conflicting sovereign directives is significant, strategists must consider the question of what unique strengths and resources the potential acquisitor brings to the domestic firm.

Fourth, the most subtle judgment of strategists occurs when the foreign acquisitor has great strengths to offer and the alternative (were the foreign acquisition to be blocked) is inferior performance, competitive decline, and (ultimately) bankruptcy for the target firm.

Once again, the alternatives for the national strategist are to permit the foreign acquisition to proceed while attempting to impose performance requirements to maximize U.S. governmental clout over the subsidiary in the case of conflicting sovereign directives, *or* to attempt to arrange a "national solution" to rescue and revitalize the target company (via trade protection, preferred procurement, subsidy, R&D grants, or acquisition by national companies).

In weighing these alternatives, it is important to point out that placing prominent American citizens on the board of directors of the foreign-acquired subsidiary is a misleading, even dangerous, nonsolution to the problem of conflicting sovereign directives. Suppose, for example, the home government of the parent company disagrees with the U.S. government on the distribution of sales of output among countries, the extent of sales to individual countries, the timing of sales to individual countries, and/or the denial of sales to particular countries. In any instance in which the home

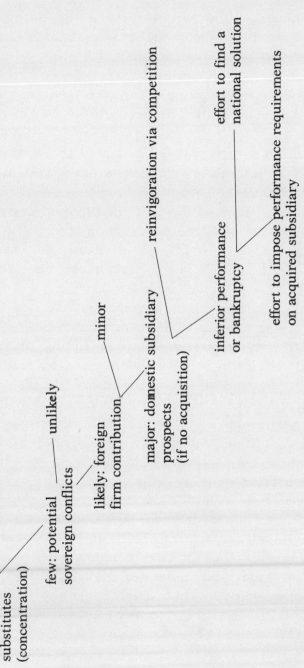

FIGURE 2. NATIONAL STRATEGY DECISION CHAIN FOR FOREIGN ACQUISITION OF DOMESTIC DEFENSE COMPANIES

government of the parent company proposes a greater number or faster pace of sales than the U.S. government, the American board members would have a fiduciary responsibility to choose the former over the latter, rendering them what Graham and Krugman have called a "fifth column" in the American midst.[65]

Within the framework illustrated above, some cases will turn out to be easier for national strategists to dissect than others. In the controversial proposed acquisition of the LTV missile business by Thomson-CSF of France, for example, the principal product lines involved (the MLRS multiple rocket launcher, the ATACM longer range rocket launcher, the ERINT anti-tactical missile interceptor, and the LOSAT anti-tank missile system) have few or no comparable substitutes. The potential for sovereign conflict over the size, distribution, timing, and/or denial of sales in various regions between France and the United States is, on the basis of the historical record, substantial, and it is exacerbated by the French government's 58 percent ownership stake in Thomson-CSF. (Thomson sales to Libya and Iraq have provoked particular controversy, in part because a Thomson-built Crotale missile shot down the one U.S. plane lost in the 1986 bombing raid on Tripoli, and Thomson radar was used to provide Iraq with advance warning in the gulf war.)[66] As for the contribution of the foreign acquisitor, it is the LTV division that possesses the technological strengths, whereas Thomson-CSF, perhaps subsidized by the French government, provides mostly capital (Thomson-CSF does supply the seeker transceiver hardware for several of the systems). While the LTV company has undergone bankruptcy proceedings due to unfunded pension liabilities in its steel operations, there is a readily available "national solution" available in the form of (lower unsubsidized) counter bids for the company from various U.S. firms. Under these circumstances, U.S. interests would be better served by following the "national solution" alternative than by permitting the Thomson-CSF acquisition to proceed with performance requirements attached.[67]

Other cases will be much less clear-cut. Some defense product lines may contain a greater number of close substitute systems. Some home governments of would-be parent corporations might have a record of closer congruence with U.S. foreign policy goals. The foreign purchasers themselves may come bearing superior technological and production skills. Moreover, as defense industries around the world shrink and rationalize operations in the face of declining military expenditures, the appeal of maintaining economies of scale via mergers across borders will grow. Finally, one should not forget that the closer integration and harmonization of defense contracting across the Atlantic and the Pacific has long been a goal of American strategists.

Here, in contrast to civilian and dual-use acquisition cases, the search for a national solution in the "close call" defense company cases probably makes good sense, with the burden of proof that the foreign acquisition better serves national interests on the shoulders of the would-be acquisitor.

Dependency and the "Golden Rule" Among Industrial Rivals

With regard to both trade and investment, the use of a concentration test to separate cases of foreign dependency that are genuinely worrisome from a national security point of view from those that are not, despite its logical consistency, provides a new challenge to American strategists: do our resulting trade and investment policies conform to the Golden Rule standard of international policymaking: namely, can we live comfortably with seeing our own policy approach being adopted by other nations as a guide to defending their own interests?[68]

In the case of foreign acquisitions, the answer is surely affirmative. The use of an objective concentration measure as a basis for rejecting or modifying proposed takeovers would be a great improvement over the vague and subjective national security justifications currently brandished in Europe and Asia. The legitimation of performance requirements as a tool of national policy around the world is not a first-best outcome, but the circumstances in which they would be permitted are narrowly and empirically defined.

In the case of trade protection in globally concentrated industries when local companies might not be able to survive on their own (or, in the case of a subsidy that replaces trade protection), the logic is no less compelling, but American readiness to accept the implications may be more problematic. American national strategists have shown a ready willingness to protect key sectors (like semiconductors) to avoid being at the mercy of foreigners. They have been equally willing to subsidize a domestic capability to generate certain crucial new-generation products (Sematech). In the future, if we were to face the prospect of having foreigners dominate the provision of, say, the next generation of semiconductors, a U.S. response that combined protection and subsidization, justified on the basis of the concentration logic introduced above, would doubtless carry great appeal.[69] But, to be consistent, we must be prepared to accept the same kind of public policies on the part of others, to pick a random example, finding others undertaking equally extraordinary measures in aerospace (Airbus). In commercial aircraft, absent public support like that given by the European sponsors of Airbus, a worldwide monopoly by Boeing (or duopoly, including a more healthy McDonnell Douglas if competition from Airbus were eliminated) is not inconceivable.[70]

In short, movement toward a rational strategy to manage the specter of foreign dependency may require the United States to abandon its hypocritical insistence that others simply let markets work when the outcome confronts them with risks we would go to great lengths to avoid ourselves.

Critical Technology Development

The desire to avoid leaving the nation's fate in the hands of external monopolists also inspires a second look at the idea of creating a civilian equivalent of DARPA (along with other public commercial technology-targeting programs).

As noted above, a strengthened R&D tax credit could accomplish most of the objectives expected of a civilian DARPA minus the drawbacks inherent in an industrial policy to which the latter would inevitably fall heir. But if we accept the argument advanced in the discussion of foreign investment that we should entice foreign firms to the United States to provide some clout over them, we find a novel rationale for creating a public R&D funding agency: we could use it as a magnet to attract foreign firms that are ahead of their U.S. counterparts to conduct R&D and carry out production on American soil. This targeting agency would invite bids from companies or groups of companies for research and development in areas drawn from a master "critical technologies" list. The list could be prepared by experts and the bids reviewed by independent anonymous referees, shielded from pork-barrel political pressures. Whether or not this kind of effort is a more efficient way of reinforcing the technology development efforts of domestic firms than the R&D tax credit, the advantage of the civilian DARPA initiative would come from inducing foreign, as well as U.S., firms to participate, turning the argument about Who-Is-Us? into the determination to Make-Them-Us![71]

The controversial and somewhat counterintuitive idea of inviting a company like (the European) Asea Brown Boveri to apply for U.S. public funding for superconductivity research (or allowing Sony to partake of DARPA grants for electro-optical research, or Siemens to join Sematech to participate in Sematech's development of semiconductor technology) would have to be carefully explained. But, an outcome in which foreign technology leaders are integrated into the U.S. industrial base—where American authorities can exercise some leverage over them (if need be)—is, from the point of view of the national strategist, far superior to the alternative of having them develop in concentrated structures offshore.

The requirement that all recipients of funding from a civilian DARPA (whether U.S. or foreign firms) engage in research, development, and manufacturing within the United States would not be an ideal outcome in terms of economic efficiency. But, as with foreign acquisitions in globally concentrated industries, performance requirements of this sort are quite likely to be a second-best stance that public authorities around the world will insist upon for the expenditure of their tax dollars. In this context, a civilian DARPA initiative could be used to obtain reciprocal access for American companies to the publicly funded technology programs of other nations.[72] The end result might be to engender some duplication of facilities around the globe as high-tech companies established R&D facilities in each of the principal industrial markets, but this is a trend that is occurring anyway.

Transnational Corporate Alliances

We cannot complete the analysis of the threat from foreign monopolists without examining one of the most delicate areas of all, the growing number of cross-border alliances among cutting-edge firms. Might the corporate agreements among high-tech companies of diverse national origins, including American origin, serve the private interests of the firms themselves but not the broader U.S. interest?

There is a fear, expressed most recently in the controversies surrounding the McDonnell Douglas–Taiwan Aerospace arrangement, that the foreign partners are taking advantage of the U.S. government's liberal attitude toward corporate alliances to exploit U.S. technological assets with the goal of pursuing a far more threatening strategy of their own in the future.[73] Instead of acting as partners, these firms could be predators, for whom cross-border relationships are simply one step in a deliberate effort to supplant and ruin their erstwhile U.S. associates. Furthermore, some observers worry that although the American prime contractors in such alliances might maintain their own market positions well enough, they might do so at the price of selling out the lesser U.S. subcontractors by offering coproduction and offset agreements to secure their larger transborder deals.

In general, the history of transborder alliances among high-tech firms is reassuring. As technological capabilities spread around the globe, American companies are treating external R&D as a resource to be tapped. The reverse transfer of technology from overseas to U.S.–based parent companies has been growing substantially in volume and importance over the past two decades, according to the National Science Foundation.[74] Transborder alliances are one embodiment of the process of obtaining access to foreign technology. Equally important, however, such alliances serve to line up supporters and neutralize opposition precisely in those industries where strategic trade theory predicts there will be strong pressures for preferential national procurement. The aerospace industry has been a pioneer in this tactic. From time to time, Boeing and Airbus have matched each other in sourcing as much as 50 percent of the content of their products in target markets. As the president of Boeing explains, "If we were to bleed off all of the aerospace production, we'd get a backlash that would cause more trouble than sharing to a degree."[75]

With regard to the concern that corporate planners may be insufficiently vigilant in protecting themselves from the ambitions of their foreign partners, the evidence from the best researched sector, aerospace, suggests that American companies, like other firms, are developing sophisticated techniques to prevent their partners from becoming full-blown rivals.[76] They circumscribe access to design and testing procedures for a given product, and maintain control over systems integration, rendering it difficult for subcontractors to use knowledge gained from one project to leapfrog the existing prime contractor and strike out on their own to develop the next generation of products.

In fact, an argument can be made that joint ventures (including joint ventures across borders) strengthen the lead firm's position for the next round of competition by enabling it to use current technology as a "cash cow" for the development of the subsequent generation. Moreover, transnational alliances help both firms and governments to spread risk and avoid "betting the company" or "betting the national champion" on a single production venture. For a broad array of reasons (technological access, market penetration, cash generation, risk reduction), therefore, national strategists would probably conclude that U.S. interests would not be served by discouraging multinational corporate alliances.

Nonetheless, the concern about the fate of sub-tier suppliers remains. Private corporate arrangements that are of benefit to American primes may come at the expense of coproduction or offset agreements that leave foreigners in a position of market domination in the subtiers. Suppose, for example, that an aerospace alliance hinges on the demand by prospective Asian partners that most of the avionics be developed and produced in Asia (a demand perhaps not unreasonable in terms of comparative costs), or that a computer alliance involving joint development of 256-megabit chips contains a stipulation that the output be fabricated in Germany and Japan. It is not at all inconceivable that the United States could find key subsectors of its industrial base being reconstituted in concentrated form abroad as a result of such private bargains.

In these circumstances, the national strategist might want to require corporations contemplating major transborder production alliances to file an "economic security impact statement" confirming that the proposed agreements did not leave the United States at the mercy of monopolistic external suppliers. The drawback to such a requirement would be the insertion of the U.S. government into the midst of private deliberations, with intrusive and possibly chilling effects. On the other hand, if the "economic security impact statement" were carefully limited to the implications of the arrangement for the structure of subcontracting industries, the result should not be far different from antitrust considerations already present in management decision-making.

Managing Dependency in an Era
of Industrial Globalization

The globalization of the industrial base in all major economies is certain to increase over the coming decades. The overall impact of this spread of products, inputs, services, technologies, and capital will be greatly beneficial. The cases that are genuinely worrisome from a national security point of view will be few, exceptional, and limited to critical industries (in which the cost to society of forgoing their output is high and the task of shifting to substitutes difficult and time-consuming) whose international structure remains concentrated.

Figure 3 summarizes the arguments above regarding trade, foreign acquisitions, public technology-targeting programs, and supervisory provisions in transborder corporate alliances. All the major industrial powers will benefit by redeploying the energy and resources traditionally devoted to cases in the B category to deal in a common, parallel way with the far fewer cases in the A category.

Once again, it is important to note the extent to which the severity of U.S. dependence on external monopolistic suppliers rests upon national action or inaction to respond to the threats discussed above. With external trade and investment accounts badly out of alignment, and with weakening and shrinking American capabilities in high-skill, high-value-added, high-tech sectors, the likelihood of finding our autonomy curtailed and our behavior manipulated by external sources will grow. With savings and consumption maintained in more disciplined proportions, and with American capabilities in high-skill,

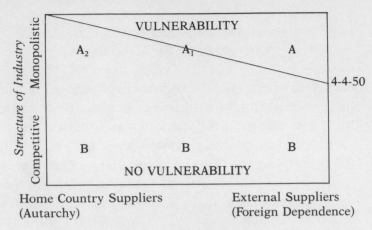

A = Exposure to the threat of delay, denial, or manipulation if trade competition in a concentrated global industry is allowed to destroy domestic producers, or if foreign acquisition is rejected and foreign suppliers of superior technology remain offshore, or if transborder corporate alliances shift subtier suppliers in concentrated industries

A_1 = Added clout to offset threat of delay, denial, or manipulation via performance requirements on foreign acquisitors, or public technology grants to induce foreign R&D (and production) on national soil.

A_2 = A successful "national solution" via revitalizing domestic-owned alternatives to foreign corporations, or via adopting provisions to ensure a portion of subtier contracts in transborder corporate alliances remain at home in concentrated supplier industries.

B = Absence of national security concerns about the location of suppliers if global industries are widely dispersed by country and company.

FIGURE 3. NATIONAL SECURITY VULNERABILITY
(EXPOSURE TO THREAT OF DELAY, DENIAL MANIPULATION)

high-value-added, high-tech industries strengthened by a solid stream of investment in R&D, plant and equipment, and human resources, there will doubtless still be some critical dependencies for the American economy, but they will much more likely be accompanied by offsetting axes of dependence where foreigners rely upon products and technologies in which the United States predominates.

IV

CONCLUSIONS

From Tactics, to Strategy,
to Grand Strategy

We began by asking whether national strategists will have to face serious threats caused by mismanagement of the domestic economy in the coming era. The answer is not only affirmative but unexpectedly somber. After reviewing the prospects for cumulative economic decline, loss of indigenous economic and technological capabilities, and growing vulnerability to external manipulation, it becomes clear that American economic policy and American national security policy are intimately linked.

In the most basic sense, the question "Is the United States in decline?" does not require a complicated and speculative response. The answer is yes. Future historians will improve upon the analytic lens of Paul Kennedy and judge this period in the last quarter of the twentieth century to have been crucial in determining America's role in the international system. If the relationship between consumption, savings, and investment proceeds unchanged, the United States will indeed follow, in its own way, the trajectory along which other great powers have slid before. In the process, the appeal to attributes of "soft power," to American values and ideas, is unlikely to halt the deterioration of America's standing in comparison to its industrial rivals or, indeed, even to maintain America's own autonomy of action, as nations look elsewhere for alliances with states that have the resources and capabilities to influence events to their own liking.

Reversing America's Decline: The Challenge of Domestic Leadership

However daunting the specter of America in decline, the direction is, at least in principle, eminently reversible. The measures needed for the epic task of solidifying America's future place in the world are not in themselves of heroic proportions. From a theoretical point of view the required macroeconomic steps (constraining consumption, rewarding savings and investment, reducing the federal budget deficit)[77] are relatively straightforward. The difficulty springs from the political task of putting them into place. The challenge for American policymakers has been transformed (and rendered more difficult, ironically) by the end of the cold war. Today, in the comforting absence of clear and present dangers, there appears to be less need for uncomfortable solutions that require discipline, sacrifice, and concerted purpose. To the popular mind the connection between threat and remedy on issues of domestic economic management and national security is obscure and the need for self-denial opaque. As a consequence, national strategists cannot assume that either the leaders or the led will turn away from short-term temptations, assume burdens, and take a long-run perspective. Instead a propensity for short-term, narrow, and self-interested action, along with a temptation to draw down on the nation's accumulated assets, poses new challenges to domestic leadership—challenges that the American political system may be ill-equipped to deal with.

Suppose, however, that American leaders and institutions can rise to the challenge of turning around the underlying deterioration of the United States' economic position, of changing the balance between consumption and savings, of investing in the country's future: what direction should national strategists then choose for trade, foreign investment, technology development, and transborder corporate alliances?

The preceding analysis, issue by issue, demonstrates that the extremes, a laissez-faire attitude of merely letting markets work and a dirigiste preference for crass versions of industrial policy and trade protection, do not, in either case, adequately serve American interests.

Less extreme, however, there are two complexes of policy response, two packages of policy approaches, that coalesce in each case with a reasonably coherent internal logic. The crucial decisions for national strategists are not only how interventionist the U.S. stance should be, but also how protectionist (in terms of trade), how exclusionary (in terms of foreign investment and foreign acquisitions), and how exclusive (in terms of technology creation).

Sophisticated Neomercantilism

The first policy complex might with some justification be called a sophisticated neomercantilism since it is constructed around preferences for having "our own" firms serve "our own" national needs first. At the margin, at least, this effort would resist Who-Is-Us? indifference to national ownership and eschew mutual gains when relative gains were available. The objective would be to maximize the presence of American-owned companies in high-value-added, technologically advanced industries around the world with the most crucial stages and most desirable jobs sited (to the extent feasible) within the United States itself.

On trade, strategists following the sophisticated neo-mercantilist approach would pursue trade-policy-as-industrial-policy proposals, using carefully crafted managed-trade arrangements (in particular, "voluntary" import expansion agreements) to allow strategic trade-type industries to penetrate external markets and tough, swift penalties to protect American producers against unfair practices (unilaterally defined) in our own markets. The methods of ensuring compliance would be to retaliate against countries where U.S. sales fell short of quantitative goals and to penalize foreign firms that did not meet America's arbitrary standards on dumping and subsidies.

On foreign investment and foreign acquisitions, this approach would involve careful scrutiny of all prospective investors, with a presumption that an acquisition would be blocked if the industry were important to national security (policymakers would be allowed broad discretion in defining national security and would be permitted to use trade protection cum subsidies to bolster failing acquisition target firms).

On technology development, American companies only need apply; the targeting of public funds would aim (in a world in which the U.S. admittedly cannot be superior in everything) at ensuring a head start for American "national champion" companies in each critical technology area. To strengthen American prospects, government support would extend relatively far into the creation of prototypes and the preparation for commercial launch of specific products.

On transborder corporate alliances, there would be restrictive governmental supervision aimed at guarding American supremacy not only at the level of prime contractors, but also at the level of subtier suppliers (as far as possible).

The designing of American policies along neo-mercantilist lines need not be crude. It cannot be said to be irrelevant. It would represent a logical response to real threats. It would look first to national self-interest, rather than to common international interest, to assure American firms and workers of the largest possible share of the most desirable economic activities.

The alternative policy complex is not simple laissez-faire. On the contrary, the more exact characterization of this policy package turns out to be somewhat surprising.

Transnational Integration

The closer we examine the alternatives in each of the areas of concern to national strategists and add them together, the clearer it becomes that the second approach would lead steadily and surely toward the integration of corporate strategies and public policies across borders.

On trade, policymakers would pursue trade liberalization along multilateral lines, with common rules for fair play and closer harmonization of national subsidy and national antitrust practices on a higher level to ensure against predation.[78] National security exceptions to free trade (via tariffs) would be narrowly specified, according to empirical criteria using concentration rules.

On foreign investment and foreign acquisitions, outsiders would be welcomed except in narrow circumstances (objectively, not discretionarily, defined), with performance requirements to enmesh foreign companies in the U.S. industrial base being the preferred remedy in the case of globally concentrated industries. Foreigners would be ensnared, not excluded.

On technology development, the principal stimulus, an expanded R&D tax credit, would be available to all firms in the domestic market, including (of course) subsidiaries of foreign corporations. A civilian DARPA to target critical technologies, far from excluding foreigners, would utilize government funding explicitly to draw leading foreign firms into the midst of the American industrial base. On Golden Rule grounds, the United States would expect and encourage other nations to do the same, thereby mitigating the exclusivity and relative advantage that any one nation's technology program might generate.[79]

On transborder corporate alliances, public policy would incorporate a presumption in favor of encouraging such alliances in recognition of the role coproduction agreements and partnerships play in assuring access to markets that otherwise are subject to pressures for nationalistic exclusivity. Safeguards against subjecting one nation or another to external monopoly would be designed to be as unobtrusive as possible, and developed in line with the international merging of antitrust practices indicated above. Ultimately, an international code might govern the exercise of extraterritorial political dictates as well as external monopolistic practices in globally concentrated industries.[80]

This second policy complex is also a logical response to real threats. It represents an attempt to modify market forces to enhance the likelihood of mutual, rather than relative, gains. This approach leads explicitly in the direction of creating mutual dependencies and cross-penetrations among the major industrial powers, even at the risk of surrendering control of domestic economic policies over time to multilateral mechanisms of supervision. Where this web of economic and technological relationships might end would require the supranational speculations of a modern-day Jean Monnet or Robert Schuman.

America's Grand Strategy:
A Future Different from the Past?

In each of the two policy complexes outlined above, the whole is greater than the sum of the parts, the first leading toward a more self-centered nationalistic structure for the international system, the second

Public Policy Approach

Policy Area	Sophisticated Neomercantilism	Transnational Integration
Trade	Selective managed trade in high-tech industries; unilateral dictation of standards for unfair trade and national security exceptions (broadly and intuitively defined)	Progressive liberalization, with common rules for fairness based on antitrust harmonization; narrow, objectively, and multilaterally defined exceptions for national security
Foreign Acquisitions	Sweeping discretionary screening of foreign acquisitions, with acquisition blocked in national security cases and target firms awarded trade protection/ subsidies	Who-Is-Us? indifference to foreign acquisitions, except for limited national security cases requiring integration of foreigners more deeply in the national industrial base
Technology Development	Large programs; U.S. firms only eligible; prototyping and prelaunch commercial assistance	Smaller programs; attraction of foreign firms to participate; early precommercial generic assistance
Transborder Corporate Alliances	Supervision and restriction of transborder alliances among primes, and protection of subtiers	Hands off (or even encouragement) of transborder alliances among primes, with safeguards for the displacement of subtiers in globally concentrated industries

FIGURE 4

toward a more transnationally integrated international system.

In which direction should national strategists head?

The answer to this question is unlikely to be found by following economic criteria alone. The technical assessment of the component proposals in each approach, sophisticated neomercantilism or transnational integration, will not permit national strategists to choose between the policies with confidence. Can voluntary import expansion agreements really be designed to make managed trade preferable to the free trade alternative? Will performance requirements truly be able to neutralize the threat from foreign acquisitions of U.S. firms in globally concentrated industries? Can Boeing or McDonnell Douglas, for example, be counted on to prevent the transfer of American avionics capabilities to foreign shores, without U.S. government supervision? National strategists will not find conclusive answers.

The supra-economic implications of pursuing one course rather than the other, in contrast, are rather clear.

To advance along the sophisticated neomercantilist path, national strategists would have to adopt unilateral and arbitrary measures to fortify the predominance of U.S. firms and production sites in key industries (imposed import quotas, blocked acquisitions, exclusive technology-development programs, dictated standards for subsidies and dumping) that would ultimately depend on the threat of denying access to the American market to be accepted. This approach would deliberately run risks of generating political divisiveness in the international arena, including mirror-image reaction and possible mutual retaliation, to bolster the relative position of American firms and workers. In short, this approach would constitute a nonmilitary equivalent of coercive diplomacy. It would have to rely on the very size and centrality of the American economy as a backstop against systemic disintegration, and count on European and Asian leaders to mute popular reaction against U.S. unilateralism out of long-term self-interest in maintaining entry into American markets (rather than, perhaps, creating more exclusive economic blocs among themselves). At the same time, to be effective in pursuing this route, national strategists would have to assure themselves that the American political system could adhere to the sophisticated neomercantilist practices outlined above and not slide into more primitive and economically counterproductive versions.

The transnational integration path also involves some delicate noneconomic assumptions. While much more conducive to international harmony, of course, it would require national strategists to keep the United States in a system-maintenance role, bearing a disproportionate share of the burdens, tolerating a certain amount of free-riding by others, taking the long-term view as the major powers struggled toward common multilateral rules on trade, investment, technology development, subsidies and dumping, and transborder corporate alliances. While the preceding analysis has shown that the nation can take out insurance policies against the worst threats that might crop up during this slow-moving process at relatively small cost to either economic efficiency or interstate tension (using concentration rules to delineate security problems), national strategists would want to assure themselves that the American political system could continue to tolerate the strains of playing the part of world leader in the interim.

Thus, in creating a grand strategy for the new era, the vision national strategists have for the future structure of the international system, and the confidence they have that national leaders will be able to move their publics toward that vision, will predominate in the choice of policy approach.

Here, once again, the macroeconomic setting reemerges in importance. In an environment of progress toward broad macroeconomic realignment in the United States (higher savings, lower consumption, greater investment, lower cost of capital for American firms), the risks of pursuing the slower, more integrative, multilateral path would be fewer than they are today. Strategic high-tech sectors in the United States would be in a stronger position to compete on their own, with lower costs, deeper pockets, and longer time horizons. They would be more resilient against whatever fair or unfair practices they met in the marketplace as cooperative efforts to level the playing field were being pursued. The threats of losing large chunks of high-value-added, technologically advanced economic activity to other nations, or of facing mounting dependencies in critical sectors, would diminish.

In an environment of little progress toward macroeconomic realignment, the need to shore up U.S. high-tech sectors via exceptional measures would be greater: these sectors (like others) would have shallower pockets and shorter time horizons and higher cost structures. Even with the fullest array of nationally self-interested efforts that sophisticated neomercantilists could promise, however, American firms and workers would still have to compete with an unfair burden imposed on them by their own society.

Most worrisome is the possibility that nationally self-interested measures may come to be used as substitutes for the fundamental changes in American behavior needed to reverse the country's decline.

The worst of all worlds would be for neomercantilistic economic policies to take the place of (or even relieve the pressure for) progress in rebalancing America's own mix of savings, consumption, and investment. The result would be a deterioration of the United States' position in the international system that would persist no matter how hard we twisted arms or threatened retaliation, accompanied by mounting tensions within the publics of various nations who were caught in the cycle of reciprocal blaming and scapegoating.[81]

Should such tensions extend over a decade or two further into the future, with new generations of citizens growing up in their midst, the world could end up looking like a much different place from today, and a far more familiar place to those acquainted with the antagonisms among great powers and their rivals of previous eras.

NOTES

Introduction

1. Since the relationship between economics and national security is extremely broad, the analysis here is confined to policies that affect the health and structure of the domestic economy, leaving aside other subjects like export controls and economic sanctions.

Chapter I

2. Paul Kennedy, *The Rise and Fall of the Great Powers* (New York: Random House, 1987), p. 529.
3. Joseph S. Nye, Jr., *Bound to Lead: The Changing Nature of American Power* (New York: Basic Books, 1991), pp. 7, 174, 260.
4. Samuel P. Huntington, "The U.S.—Decline or Renewal?" *Foreign Affairs* 67 (Winter 1988/89), p. 95.
5. Martin Feldstein and Phillipe Bacchetta calculate that, in the short run, capital inflows compensate nearly totally for a decline in national savings, but over the longer run downward movements in national savings lead to nearly equal (70–86 percent) reductions in domestic investment ("National Saving and International Investment," in B. Douglas Bernheim and John B. Shoven, eds., *National Saving and Economic Performance* [Chicago: University of Chicago Press, 1991]), pp. 201–26.
6. It is necessary to differentiate between capital flows in general (whereby foreigners make a comparatively "passive" purchase of an asset that generates a rate of return, like bonds or commercial paper or a portfolio of equities) and direct investment by non-American companies to build or acquire productive facilities. The pace and magnitude of

the latter is much harder to predict than that of the former. Direct foreign investment will receive more detailed treatment in the section on Threat III.

7. The first annual report to the president and Congress by the Competitiveness Policy Council points out that the United States increased its debt much faster over the last decade than it did to finance World War II. See *Building a Competitive America* (Washington, D.C.: Competitiveness Policy Council, March 1, 1992), p. 13.

8. Since the late 1980s, foreign capital inflows have tapered off (see note 5). The low U.S. savings rate leaves American national strategists in a quandary: higher foreign capital inflows open up the prospect of foreign influence and foreign control; lower foreign capital inflows mean fewer resources to improve American productivity, innovation, and output. For further exploration of these issues, including the Who-Is-Us? question about direct foreign investment, see the treatment of Threat III (dependency).

9. A "Made in America" label for the trade deficit does not exonerate others from the charge of unfair trade practices. For evidence that Japan, for example, is packing its trade surplus with high-tech products, so to speak, see Table 4.

10. Koichi Hamada and Kasumasa Iwata, "On the International Capital Ownership Pattern at the Turn of the Twenty-First Century," *European Economic Review* 33 (1989), pp. 1055–85.

11. Thus, even with a shift of resources away from military spending, as Kennedy advocates, the decline in relative economic performance will persist so long as the "peace dividend" is not itself invested in productive uses, whether or not the "nonproductive" consumption comes in a socially appealing form, like improved health care for the elderly poor.

Chapter II

12. Martin Neil Baily and Alok K. Chakrabarti, *Innovation and the Productivity Crisis* (Washington, D.C.: The Brookings Institution, 1988), p. 9. For comparisons of U.S.–Japanese productivity in 29 specific industries, see Dale W. Jorgenson and Masahiro Kuroda, *Productivity and International Competitiveness in Japan and the United States, 1960–1985*, dis-

tributed by the National Academy of Sciences, October 24, 1991.

13. One might want to add investment in public infrastructure as well. Between 1980 and 1989 (the latest figures available on a comparative basis), net government investment as a percentage of gross domestic product was 5.7 percent for Japan, 4.8 percent for Italy, 3.7 percent for Germany, 2.0 percent for Britain, 1.8 percent for Canada, and 0.3 percent for the United States (OECD data), (*New York Times*, January 27, 1992). For the analysis of investment and productivity, see Edward F. Denison, *Trends in American Economic Growth, 1929–1982* (Washington, D.C.: The Brookings Institution, 1985); Edward A. Hudson and Dale W. Jorgenson, "U.S. Energy Policy and Economic Growth, 1975–2000," *Bell Journal of Economics and Management Science* 5 (Autumn 1974), pp. 456–62; Barry P. Bosworth, "Capital Formation and Economic Policy," *Brookings Papers on Economic Activity* 2 (1982); Baily and Chakrabarti, *Innovation and the Productivity Crisis*; Michael F. Mohr, *Diagnosing the Productivity Problem and Developing an Rx for Improving the Prognosis* (Washington, D.C.: Cabinet Council for Economic Affairs, October 1983, unpublished; cited in Baily and Chakrabarti, p. 22); and Ralph Landau, "Capital Investment: Key to Competitiveness and Growth," *The Brookings Review* 8 (Summer 1990). Leaving aside investment in human capital for a moment, all of these analyses show the importance of three categories whose boundaries are difficult to delineate precisely: investment in plant and equipment, investment in pushing out the technological frontier, and investment in diffusing technology once it has been developed. Each of these three categories is sensitive to the cost of capital and the time horizon differential highlighted here. More broadly, Jorgenson and Kuroda have found increases in capital input to be the most important source of economic growth in both the United States and Japan, accounting for as much as 40 percent of U.S. growth and 60 percent of Japanese growth (*Productivity and International Competitiveness in Japan and the United States*). When labor is added, Jorgenson finds that three-fourths of all U.S. economic growth during the 1948–1979 period is accounted for by increases in capital and labor inputs (Dale W. Jorgenson, "Productivity and Postwar U.S. Economic Growth," *Journal of Economic Perspectives* 2 [Fall 1988], pp. 23–41).

14. In general, the integration of capital markets across borders should lead cost of capital differentials to disappear. In this

vein, Jeffrey Frankel argues, for example, that whereas the cost of capital was lower in Japan than in the United States in the 1970s and the 1980s (due to the high Japanese savings rates), in the 1990s the cost of capital may rise to U.S. rates. Frankel acknowledges that real differences have been perpetuated in the U.S.–Japanese case, despite international arbitrage. As indicated in the text, there are two reasons why the Japanese capital market may remain somewhat segmented, however. First, the integration of capital markets cannot be complete without the integration of product markets as well: borrowing in yen at a cheaper rate than borrowing dollars requires the assumption of an obligation to repay in yen; for American firms (General Motors, Motorola) this requires confidence that borrowers can earn yen to repay the loan by selling products in Japan. If firms lack that confidence, they are effectively denied the ability to assume the yen liability. Second, cost of capital differences are maintained by the inability of American firms to acquire companies in Japan. A net advantage accrues to those firms that have to pay out less to stockholders (and perhaps to lenders as well) if both are willing to accept a lower rate of return. Ordinarily, the prospect of hostile takeovers would keep firms from squeezing shareholders and creditors in this way. Thus, the conspicuous absence in Japan of hostile takeovers by non-Japanese investors helps Japanese firms maintain a lower cost in financing their operations. In addition, as discussed below, the unusual behavior of the United States in imposing double taxation on earnings from capital, whether by taxing dividends twice or by imposing a capital gains tax on retained earnings that show up as gains in share prices, raises the cost of capital to American companies. See Jeffrey A. Frankel, "The Japanese Cost of Finance: A Survey," *Financial Management* (Spring 1991), pp. 95–127. For a skeptical view about cost of capital differences, see W. Carl Kester and Timothy A. Luehrman, "Cross-Country Differences in the Cost of Capital: A Survey and Evaluation of Recent Empirical Studies," unpublished, prepared for the U.S. Council on Competitiveness, May 1991.

15. Benjamin Friedman calculates that the real rate of interest rose from an average of eight-tenths of 1 percent (1951–1980) to 4.7 percent (1981–1990) ("Learning from the Reagan Deficits," unpublished draft 1992). Robert Lawrence has found that macroeconomic volatility may also affect the time horizons of U.S. managers (variable inflation

rates, sluggish growth rates, fluctuating exchange rates). See *Building A Competitive America*, p. 12.

16. Juliet B. Schor, *The Overworked Americans: The Unexpected Decline of Leisure* (New York: Basic Books, 1992).

17. Congressional Budget Office, *Educational Achievement: Explanations and Implications of Recent Trends* (Washington, D.C.: GPO, 1987); Mark Dynarski, "The Scholastic Aptitude Test: Participation and Performance," *Economics of Education Review* 6 (1987), pp. 263–273; Eric A. Hanushek and Lori L. Taylor, "Alternative Assessments of the Performance of Schools, *The Journal of Human Resources* 25 (1990), pp. 179–201. The latter shows that achievement growth, or value added over time, is by far the superior measurement of school quality differences.

18. "National Assessment of Vocational Education," Testimony of John G. Wirt, Lana Muraskin, Robert Meyer, and David Goodman before the House Education and Labor Committee, March 7, 1989, *Economics of Education Review* 8 (1989), pp. 383–92; Jim Bishop, "Incentives for Learning: Why American High School Students Compare So Poorly to Their Counterparts Overseas," *Labor Economics* 11 (1990), pp. 17–51.

19. *America's Choice: high skills or low wages!* The Report of the Commission on the Skills of the American Workforce (Rochester, N.Y.: National Center on Education and the Economy, June 1990), Chapter 6 and Supporting Information IV: Skills Investment Taxes: Foreign Examples.

20. See Lawrence Mishel and Ruy A. Teixeira, "Behind the Numbers: The Myth of the Coming Labor Shortage," *The American Prospect* 4 (Fall 1991), pp. 98–103.

21. A similar case can be made for "defense industry conversion" adjustment assistance to speed the shift of employment from military-related to civilian occupations. See Theodore H. Moran, *Managing the Defense Industrial Base in an Era of Lower Defense Budgets* (Washington, D.C.: Center for Strategic and International Studies, forthcoming 1992).

22. On the other hand, according to the *Wall Street Journal*, "the Labor Department is making a renewed attempt to repeal trade-adjustment assistance," (January 31, 1992). For the design of more effective trade adjustment assistance policies, see Robert Z. Lawrence and Robert E. Litan, *Saving Free Trade: A Pragmatic Approach* (Washington, D.C.: The Brookings Institution, 1986).

23. See the study reported by Robert E. Lipsey and Irving B. Kravis, "Sorting Out the Trade Problem," *New York Times*, January 18, 1987.

24. For the comparison of assets per worker in domestic versus overseas manufacturing operations, see Laura D'Andrea Tyson, "They Are Not Us: Why American Ownership Still Matters," *The American Prospect* 4 (Winter 1991), pp. 37–53. In general, Lipsey and Weiss have found that the higher a U.S. firm's output in a foreign area, the larger its exports from the U.S. to that area. This relationship is particularly strong between foreign output and exports of intermediate goods for further processing (Robert E. Lipsey and Merle Yahr Weiss, "Foreign Production and Exports of Individual Firms," *The Review of Economics and Statistics* 63 [May 1984], pp. 304–308). See also C. Fred Bergsten, Thomas Horst, and Theodore Moran, *American Multinationals and American Interests* (Washington, D.C.: The Brookings Institution, 1978), Chapter 3.

25. Andrew M. Warner, "Does World Investment Demand Determine U.S. Exports?" International Finance Discussion Papers of the Federal Reserve Board, No. 423, 1992.

26. *Washington Post*, January 22, 1991.

27. Advice cited with ridicule by Robert Kuttner, *The End of Laissez-Faire* (New York: Alfred A. Knopf, 1991), p. 113.

28. *The Highest Stakes: The Economic Foundations of the New Security System* (Berkeley, Cal.: The Berkeley Roundtable on International Economics, draft 1992).

29. See *Industrial Change and Public Policy* (Kansas City: The Federal Reserve Bank of Kansas City, 1983), Chapter 4. This analytic helps sort out the argument that the United States already has an industrial policy; the objective should be to rationalize it and do it right. Those public spending programs that supply resources where the social benefits far exceed what private markets would appropriate (e.g., the agricultural extension service, the public highway system) are clearly justified. Those public spending programs that merely allocate resources differently from how the market would supply them (e.g., investment tax credits that favor the rustbelt but not software development or cad/cam engineering services) are not.

30. Baily and Chakrabarti, *Innovation and the Productivity Crisis*; Gene M. Grossman, "Promoting New Industrial Activities: A Survey of Recent Arguments and Evidence," *OECD Economic Studies* 14 (Spring 1990), pp. 87–125; Linda R. Cohen and Roger G. Noll, *The Technology Pork-*

88—AMERICAN ECONOMIC POLICY AND NATIONAL SECURITY

barrel (Washington, D.C.: The Brookings Institution, 1991);
Manuel Trajtenberg, "The Welfare Analysis of Product
Innovations, with an Application to Computed Tomography
Scanners," *Journal of Political Economy* 97 (1989),
pp. 444–79.

31. For a comprehensively muddled compilation of the pros
and cons of a governmental or quasi-governmental civilian
technology agency, see the report of the Panel on the Government Role in Civilian Technology, *The Government Role
in Civilian Technology: Building a New Alliance* (Washington, D.C.: National Academy Press, 1992). One might want
to make the R&D tax credit more readily applicable to
expenditures involving participation in consortia of corporations, although the evidence from efforts at joint R&D
development has not proved to be as positive as once hoped
(either in the United States or abroad, e.g., Japan). For
debate about the use of the R&D tax credit and ways to
improve its efficacy, see Edwin Mansfield, "Statement to
the House Ways and Means Committee on the Effects of the
R&D Tax Credit," August 2–3, 1984; Baily and Chakrabarti,
Innovation and the Productivity Crisis; and David L. Brum-
baugh, "The Research and Experimentation Tax Credit"
(Washington, D.C.: Library of Congress, Congressional Research Service Issue Brief, May 9, 1991).

32. Adam B. Jaffee, "Technological Opportunity and Spillovers
of R&D: Evidence from Firm's Patents, Profits, and Market
Value," *American Economic Review* 76 (1986), pp. 984–99.
Baily and Chakrabarti (using a different classification) find
five industries accounting for 86 percent of all company
funded R&D. The industries are transportation equipment,
electrical machinery, nonelectrical machinery, chemicals,
and instruments (*Innovation and the Productivity Crisis*, Table 6-1, p. 124). One would also want to provide a stimulus
to the 60–65 percent of all smaller manufacturers who have
not even adapted the most basic computer-aided design or
numerically guided equipment to their operations. U.S.
General Accounting Office, *Technology Transfer: Federal Efforts to Enhance the Competitiveness of Small Manufacturers*
(Washington, D.C.: General Accounting Office, November
1991).

33. Zvi Griliches, "Productivity, R&D, and Basic Research at
the Firm Level in the 1970s," *American Economic Review* 76
(1986), pp. 141-54; F. R. Lichtenberg and D. Siegel, "The
Impact of R&D Investment on Productivity: New Evidence
Using Linked R&D–LRD Data," Working Paper No. 2901

(1989), National Bureau of Economic Research. Findings such as this suggest that expanding and strengthening the R&D tax credit may in fact do more to encourage process R&D and speed diffusion of industry "best practices" to smaller subtier firms than the more popular manufacturing technology centers, technology extension programs, and regional technology alliances. One cannot help wishing that there were more rigorous studies of information diffusion, market imperfections, and the role of public sector "extension" or "cooperation" services. Such studies could include a comparison with U.S. agricultural extension programs, and with German and Japanese manufacturing support centers. In the end, there might be an important synergy between strengthening the R&D tax credit and expanding technology "extension service" activities. See John A. Alic, Lewis M. Branscomb, Harvey Brooks, Ashton B. Carter, Gerald L. Epstein, *Beyond Spinoff: Military and Commercial Technologies in a Changing World* (Boston: Harvard Business School Press, 1992). A further implication is that public funds expended via the R&D tax credit would produce stronger results for the civilian sector than funds dispersed via DARPA for dual-use technologies. DARPA's comparative advantage would lie in projects that the civilian sector would otherwise not pursue (or would pursue much less vigorously) on its own. Moreover, a large proportion of DARPA's undertakings are inherently dual use, without having to channel its efforts in that direction.

34. For overviews, see Paul R. Krugman, ed., *Strategic Trade Policy and the New International Economics* (Cambridge, Mass.: MIT Press, 1986); J. David Richardson, "The Political Economy of Strategic Trade Policy," *International Organization* 44 (Winter 1990), pp. 107–35.

35. The case for public action to correct for market failure may be presumptively stronger for strategic trade-type industries: given their knowledge intensity, the generation of positive externalities for the societies where they are located might be the appropriate assumption (until demonstrated otherwise), rather than the standard economic postulate that there are no uncompensated spillovers until proven to the contrary. In order to maximize the benefits to the state where the industries are located, one must assume, in addition, that some of the externalities accrue only to the local or national population rather than being spread throughout the global market.

36. On the unexpected success of parallel processing over single-vector processing in supercomputers, see "Future of Big Computing: A Triumph for the Lilliputians," *New York Times*, November 25, 1990. In the supercomputer race, the Japanese technocratic, industrial, and bureaucratic elite bet on single-vector processing. On analog versus digital technologies for HDTV, see Cynthia A. Beltz, *High Tech Maneuvers: Industrial Policy Lessons of HDTV* (Washington, D.C.: AEI Press, 1991). The Beltz study coincides with the Japanese view of the HDTV race, where the government-owned Japan Broadcasting Corporation's "entry . . . is given very little chance of coming out on top for technical as well as political reasons" (*Japan Economic Survey* 16 [January 1992], p. 13). To be fair, success with a portfolio of projects is the appropriate yardstick for judging public policy outcomes, not success in every single project.
37. Richard G. Lipsey and Wendy Dobson, *Shaping Comparative Advantage* (Scarborough, Ontario: Prentice-Hall Canada, 1987), pp. 59, 123.
38. J. David Richardson has found that, under conditions of imperfect competition, trade liberalization leads to efficiency gains that may even run two to three times greater than those under perfect competition ("Empirical Research on Trade Liberalization with Imperfect Competition: A Survey," *OECD Economic Studies* 12 [Spring 1989], pp. 87–125).
39. David C. Mowery and Nathan Rosenberg, "New Developments in U.S. Technology Policy: Implications for Competitiveness and International Trade Policy," *California Management Review* 32 (Fall 1989), pp. 29–38. For a more "nuanced" and sympathetic appraisal of the 1986 Semiconductor Agreement, see Laura D'Andrea Tyson, *Who's Bashing Whom? Trade Conflicts in High-Technology Industries* (Washington, D.C.: Institute for International Economics, forthcoming 1992), Chapter 4.
40. Industrial policy advocates point out, with some justification, that here the preoccupation of conventional economics with consumer welfare is genuinely dissatisfying: on subsidies and dumping, the rigorous economic response is to send the perpetrator a thank-you note; on trade protection, the economic conclusion is that the offending nation is only hurting itself. See Milton Friedman, "In Defense of Dumping," in *Bright Promises, Dismal Performance: An Economist's Protest* (New York: Harcourt Brace Jovanovich, 1983). To justify a public policy of objecting to unfair trade prac-

tices, economists resort not to an examination of immediate welfare effects but to an argument that such measures on the part of some actors will produce a political reaction in others that retards the liberalization process itself and/or, in the extreme, provokes trade wars. See Jagdish Bhagwati, *Protectionism* (Cambridge, Mass.: MIT Press, 1989). But the economic complacency about how other nations favor their producers over their consumers may (in some crucial cases) be shortsighted, for the dynamic reasons concerned with gaining unilateral advantage that strategic trade theorists have highlighted.

41. Paulo Guerrieri, "Technology and International Trade Performance of the Most Advanced Countries," cited in Tyson, *Who's Bashing Whom?*, Chapter 2.

42. Kuttner, *End of Laissez-Faire*, p. 11; Prestowitz, *Hearings on the McDonnell Douglas–Taiwan Aerospace Agreement*, Joint Economic Committee, December 3, 1991.

43. Tyson, *Who's Bashing Whom?*, p. 22.

44. Success in negotiating such rules would ultimately require state, as well as federal, agencies in the United States to give up their Buy American guidelines.

45. In the EC, public purchases cover 90 percent of telecommunications equipment sales and one-third of computer sales by American companies; in Japan the percentages covered by public directives may be higher. Kenneth Flamm, "Semiconductors," in Gary Clyde Hufbauer, ed., *Europe 1992* (Washington, D.C.: The Brookings Institution, 1990), Chapter 5.

46. The attempt to place state and municipal subsidies under supranational restraints on high-tech subsidies is likely to be particularly difficult. In attempting to launch the MD-12X, for example, McDonnell Douglas has played American communities off against each other in granting benefits to secure the siting of a new aircraft plant with 10,000 or more jobs ("Towns Spare No Effort to Snare New Plant," *New York Times*, December 18, 1991).

47. U.S. trade law currently defines dumping in terms of a rather high calculation of previous average costs (imputing 10-percent administrative charges and an 8-percent profit rate). Competitive pressures will push all firms' prices toward marginal rather than average cost, however, with the former being lower than the latter frequently over the course of each business cycle (to maximize allocative efficiency national strategists should find this outcome desirable). For strategic trade-type industries, even a calculation

of current marginal cost is inappropriate since companies must invest in large production runs to be successful. This is as true for Intel and Boeing as it is for Fujitsu and Airbus. Thus, some estimates suggest that a large proportion of all high tech firms are technically "dumping," according to U.S. trade law standards, all the time. See Alan V. Deardorff, "Economic Perspectives on Dumping Law," Department of Economics, University of Michigan, Seminar Discussion Paper No. 240, February 8, 1989. For an explanation (and defense) of U.S. laws, see "Subsidies and Dumping: What They Are, Why They Matter" in *Competing Economies: America, Europe and the Pacific Rim* (Washington, D.C.: Office of Technology Assessment, 1991), pp. 138–54.

48. The Semiconductor Agreement of 1991 centered on import targets in the Japanese market and backed away from the export limitations on Japanese products needed to maintain minimum floor prices in the 1986 agreement. For a critique of VIEs, see Bhagwati, *Protectionism*, pp. 80-86. For a more sympathetic view, see Tyson, *Who's Bashing Whom?*, Chapter 1. Tyson argues that "the distinction between negotiating rules and negotiating outcomes is not as straightforward or pure as Bhagwati would have us believe" and can sometimes be used to increase competition. Moreover, as in the Moss Talks (market-oriented, sector-selective trade talks) in several technology-intensive industries in the mid-1980s, the outcome can in principle be applied to all trading partners. Finally, argues Tyson, VIEs may play a useful role in familiarizing users with imports.

49. In GATT negotiations, U.S. policy on dumping has the schizophrenic task of assisting U.S. companies to avoid being subject to unreasonable dumping charges as they attempt to compete abroad while preserving America's system of dumping laws which, in the estimation of the Department of Commerce, would be "quickly undone" if allowed to be opened to GATT scrutiny. See Labor-Industry Coalition for International Trade, *The Uruguay Round: Will It Be a Good Deal for U.S. Manufacturing?* (Washington, D.C.: LICIT, December 1991), and the LICIT pamphlet, "The Dunkel Texts and U.S. Trade Law Remedies," January 8, 1992.

50. See Ludger Schuknecht and Heinrich W. Ursprung, "Anti-Dumping Policies in the U.S. and the EC," University of Konstanz, unpublished draft 1991; Arnold and Porter, "U.S. Government Support of the U.S. Commercial Aircraft Industry," prepared for the Commission of the European Communities, Washington, D.C., November 1991.

Chapter III

51. Every sector produces some "vacuous" products in response to consumer demand. For the agribusiness/agrochemical sector, potato chips may be an example; for the microelectronics sector, perhaps pulsating Christmas tree lights would be a counterpart. The national strategist would want to compare either potato chips with pulsating Christmas tree lights (and be relatively indifferent if both were supplied from outside national borders), or microchips with bioenzymes (and wish that the nation had domestic capabilities in both). "Vacuous" means the cost to the society of doing without them is relatively low and the difficulty of shifting to substitutes is relatively easy; "critical" implies the opposite.

52. In Europe, birthplace of mercantilist and neomercantilist doctrines, the reality of having to incorporate the leading technologies, products, and processes rapidly and continuously into the national economy to keep up with rival states led to quite high levels of dependence (even in weapons systems) despite a professed preference for autarchy. See Andrew Moravcsik, "Arms and Autarchy in Modern European History," in *Searching for Security in a Global Economy, Daedalus* 120 (Fall 1991), pp. 23–47.

53. See Theodore H. Moran, "The Globalization of America's Defense Industries: Managing the Threat of Foreign Dependence," *International Security* 15 (Summer 1990), pp. 57–100.

54. "U.S. Business Access to Certain State-of-the-Art Technology" (Washington, D.C.: General Accounting Office, September 1991, NSIAD-91-278). Non-Japanese firms were not a significant component of this study.

55. The use of a concentration test in no sense implies that dependence upon external suppliers is merely an antitrust problem, or should be relegated to Justice Department jurisdiction. While the four-four-fifty rule can be operationalized in terms of the Herfindahl index and made compatible with Hart-Rodino guidelines for mergers and acquisitions, its use for national strategists lies in signaling a credible threat of denial on the part of foreign firms (or their home governments). Concentration in the global market, not the domestic market, is the relevant standard. See the report of the General Accounting Office, *Foreign Vulnerability of Critical Technologies*, forthcoming 1992. For

further discussion of concentration measures, see Edward
M. Graham and Michael E. Ebert, "Foreign Direct Investment and National Security: Fixing the Exon-Florio Process," *The World Economy* 14 (September 1991), pp. 245–268.

56. Many industry appeals for protection on national security
grounds do not formally take the Section 232 ("national
security") route in U.S. trade law.

57. From an economist's point of view, a subsidy is less distortionary than a tariff. The choice of a tariff in this analysis
reflects a judgment that, for the United States, on-budget
subsidies are less palatable politically and less feasible
fiscally than an off-budget solution. Thus, the choice of a
tariff reflects the second-best analysis of the preceding section, but avoids the third-best options of VRAs or VERs.

58. The semiconductor industry may (or may not) be a case in
point.

59. Charles L. Schultze has estimated that more than 30 percent of the trade flows among the major industrial powers is
intra-industry trade, examined at a relatively close (three-
digit) level of detail ("Industrial Policy: A Dissent," *The
Brookings Review*, 2 [Fall 1983], p. 8).

60. The data do suggest, however, that there may be higher
imports on the part of foreign subsidiaries, as well as a
propensity to buy from related companies, at least among
Japanese investors. See Edward M. Graham and Paul R.
Krugman, *Foreign Direct Investment in the United States*,
2nd edition (Washington, D.C.: Institute for International
Economics, 1991); Robert Z. Lawrence, "Efficient or Exclu-
sionist? The Import Behavior of Japanese Corporate
Groups," *Brookings Papers on Economic Activity* (1991),
pp. 311–30.

61. Robert B. Reich, "Who Is Us?" *Harvard Business Review* 90
(January-February 1990), pp. 53–64.

62. *Foreign Direct Investment in the United States* (Washington,
D.C.: U.S. Department of Commerce, June 1991). A green-
field investment in which a foreign firm set up operations
from scratch (instead of acquiring a domestic firm) and
proceeded to drive local rivals from the market would be
similarly worrisome but might be more likely to meet the
performance requirement objective (below).

63. For a similar case of proposed acquisition in which the
international industry was unduly concentrated, see the
Semigas case ("U.S. to Fight High-Tech Firm's Sale," *Washington Post*, December 29, 1990).

64. In the crucible of conflicting governmental directives U.S. firms have not infrequently put their own interests first in siding with host pressures over the dictates of their home government. There is some evidence companies from other countries (Britain, France) have done the same. But would Japanese, Korean, Taiwanese, or German firms? For evidence from the 1973 oil embargo through the Soviet gas pipeline case of 1982, see Moran, "Globalization of America's Defense Industries."

65. Graham and Krugman, *Foreign Direct Investment*, pp. 98–102.

66. "Data Sought on Thomson Deals with Libya, Iraq," *Washington Post*, April 30, 1992.

67. Reinforcing this conclusion, there would likely be a gradual shift of production and technological upgrading from the United States to France in the Thomson-CSF proposal, despite initial performance requirements. LTV's array of subcontractors already includes competitors on both sides of the Atlantic. Over time, one might expect greater levels of assembly and product improvement to be awarded to Aerospatiale, Cruesot Loire, SNP, and GIAT and less to be done by FMC, Atlantic Research, Honeywell, and Brunswick if the acquisition were allowed to proceed. The fact of French government ownership in Thomson-CSF opens the door to subsidies and other unfair pricing arrangements that could enable the French parent or its suppliers to underbid their American counterparts. See Testimony of Theodore H. Moran before the Subcommittee on Defense Industry and Technology, Senate Armed Services Committee, April 30, 1992.

68. For the idea of the Golden Rule standard, see Theodore H. Moran and David C. Mowery, "Aerospace and National Security," forthcoming 1993.

69. For a recommendation to strengthen U.S. government capabilities to "respond intelligently to proposals for assistance from specific industries" along these lines, see the Competitiveness Policy Council report, *Building a Competitive America*, p. 33.

70. Paul Krugman and Richard Baldwin have suggested that the welfare gains to Europe do not justify the cost ("Industrial Policy and International Competition in Wide Bodied Jet Aircraft," in Robert Baldwin, ed., *Trade Policy Issues and Empirical Analysis* [Chicago: University of Chicago Press, 1988], pp. 45–71). Laura Tyson has countered that Krugman and Baldwin do not adequately include the dynamic

gains from learning how to be successful in aerospace via Airbus. The analysis here suggests that to the dynamic calculation a "national security premium" to avoid the dependence-on-a-foreign-monopolist threat should be added. In the end, the Europeans might well conclude, however, that $12–$15 billion over twenty years (the amount of the subsidies to Airbus) is too much to pay.

71. I am indebted to Laura Tyson for this characterization of my argument.

72. Beyond the economic implications of such reciprocity, this "exchange of hostages" might mute the home country political impulse to issue extraterritorial diktats to offshore affiliates, as in the Soviet gas pipeline or Kyocera cases; it would also set in place a structure of interest groups disposed to resist such extraterritorial interventions.

73. See the *Hearings on the McDonnell Douglas–Taiwan Aerospace Agreement*, Joint Economic Committee, December 3, 1991. For earlier discussion of the FSX controversy, see James E. Aver, "The U.S.–Japan FSX Agreement: Cooperation or Confrontation in High Technology," *Business in the Contemporary World* 2 (Summer 1990), pp. 105–12.

74. Reported in Thomas H. Lee and Proctor P. Reid, eds., *National Interests in an Age of Global Technology* (Washington, D.C.: National Academy Press, 1991), p. 26.

75. Luis Kraar, "Boeing Takes a Bold Plunge to Keep Flying High," *Fortune*, September 25, 1980, p. 79.

76. Moran and Mowery, "Aerospace and National Security." For an in-depth discussion of corporate alliances, see Peter F. Cowhey and Jonathan D. Aronson, *Managing the World Economy: The Consequences of Corporate Alliances* (New York: Council on Foreign Relations Press, forthcoming 1993).

Chapter IV

77. On the revenue side, the United States in fact taxes its population less heavily than other industrial states. Government receipts as a percentage of gross domestic product put France at 47 percent, Germany at 45 percent, Italy at 41 percent, Britain at 40 percent, Canada at 40 percent, Japan at 33 percent, and the U.S. at 32 percent (OECD figures for 1989, the most recent available), (*New York Times*, January 27, 1992).

78. There might be tactical priority given to obtaining nationality-blind procurement practices in strategic trade-type industries (putting their needs for equal access high on the list of concessions demanded in bilateral and multilateral negotiations, to ensure against shutting one country or another out of a given generation of products) but not the quantitative demands of managed trade. It should be noted that the strategic-trade rationale for rapid results is conceptually distinct from the "cultural differences" rationale advanced by Prestowitz and Van Wolferen; for the latter, on negotiating grounds alone, the United States will gain tactical success more consistently by setting priorities among American demands rather than simply insisting that others open their markets in general (i.e. we should tell the Japanese that semiconductor sales are more important than rice sales, or vice versa, and not simply insist that free trade is a good thing), (Prestowitz, *Trading Places*; Karel G. van Wolferen, "The Japan Problem," *Foreign Affairs* 65 (Winter 1986/87), pp. 288–303).

79. The integrationist approach to extreme cases of potential global monopoly (e.g., Boeing versus Airbus) would be to allow nations the right to sponsor programs to fund domestic competitors so long as firms of all nationalities were eligible to participate.

80. For prior recommendations along these lines, see Raymond Vernon, "The Multinationals: No Strings Attached," *Foreign Policy*, No. 33 (Winter 1979), pp. 121–34.

81. The "realist" school of international relations theory predicts that as American preeminence disappears the United States will be prone to favor relative gains over mutual gains in its interactions with other industrial powers. Some members of the realist school have urged the United States deliberately to place the outcome of international negotiations at risk unless we obtain a previously specified distribution of benefits ("American national interest would be better served by a policy based on specific reciprocity, a policy that paid more attention to short-term payoffs, outcomes rather than procedures," Stephen Krasner has written. "Such a policy would not push the world down a slippery slope of growing protectionism . . . "). But in an environment of ongoing macroeconomic misalignment in the United States, a policy of trying to improve America's position vis-à-vis its major rivals by insisting on larger relative gains in international negotiations will be both economically futile and politically wearing. Indeed prompt

tit-for-tat retaliation, often recommended in game theory to discourage defection from cooperative solutions, is likely to be a recipe for escalation rather than dampening of conflict in a setting of persistent macroeconomic imbalances. For a review of the realist argument (along with mixed evidence about the extent to which the United States has actually moved toward a relative gains perspective), see Michael Mastanduno, "Do Relative Gains Matter? America's Response to Japanese Industrial Policy," *International Security* 16 (Summer 1991), pp. 67–89. For the Krasner quotation, see Stephen D. Krasner, "A Trade Strategy for the United States," *Ethics & International Affairs* 2 (1988), pp. 46–59. The broader tit-for-tat strategy to "elicit cooperation" can be found in Judith L. Goldstein and Stephen D. Krasner, "Unfair Trade Practices: The Case for a Differential Response," *American Economic Review* 74 (May 1984), pp. 282–87. Goldstein and Krasner do suggest that their tit-for-tat recommendation should be focused on violation of GATT rules and nontariff barriers covered by international agreements, but they also include antidumping as an exemplary area for more active retaliation.

ABOUT THE AUTHOR

Theodore H. Moran is Karl F. Landegger Professor and Director of the Program in International Business Diplomacy, School of Foreign Service, Georgetown University. Dr. Moran is also Professor and member of the Executive Council, Georgetown School of Business Administration.

In addition to some fifty scholarly articles, he has published nine books, including *Governments and Transnational Corporations* (forthcoming), *Investment in Development: New Rules for Private Capital?*, with contributors, (Overseas Development Council); *Multinational Corporations: The Political Economy of Foreign Direct Investment* (Lexington Books); *Managing International Political Risk: Strategies and Techniques*, ed. with Fariborz Ghadar and Stephen Kobrin (Overseas Private Investment Corporation); *American Multinationals and American Interests*, with C. Fred Bergsten and Thomas Horst (Brookings); and *Multinational Corporations and the Politics of Dependence: Copper in Chile* (Princeton University Press).

Professor Moran has taught at Harvard, Vanderbilt, the Paul H. Nitze School of Advance International Studies, and the Colorado School of Mines. He received his Ph.D. in government from Harvard in 1971. Since then he has been a consultant to corporations, governments, and multilateral agencies on investment strategy, international negotiations, and political risk assessment.

Former member of the Policy Planning Staff of the Department of State, Dr. Moran was appointed Chairman of the Pew Foundation's Economic Freedom Fellows Program in 1992, which trains emerging leaders from the former Soviet Union and other countries in the transition to market economies. In 1992 he also became a Senior Research Associate of Business Executives for National Security.

Dr. Moran's current work deals with high tech business policy, international trade and investment, and national security.